TOPSAIL SCHOONER

BARQUE

'INE

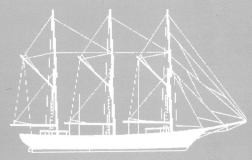

SCHOONER

GAFF CUTTER
with Topsail

NER

GAFF KETCH

Asgard

THE STORY OF IRISH SAIL TRAINING

Asgard

THE STORY OF IRISH SAIL TRAINING

WM NIXON

AND

CAPTAIN ERIC HEALY

COISTE AN ASGARD

© 2000 *Coiste an Asgard*

Also by W M Nixon

The Sailing Cruiser
Published 1977 by Nautical Publishing Co. and 1978 by Dodd, Mead of New York

To Sail the Crested Sea
Published 1979 by The Irish Cruising Club

Howth - A Centenary of Sailing
Published 1995 by Howth Yacht Club
Harbour Road, Howth, Co Dublin

Published by *Coiste an Asgard*
Infirmary Road,
Dublin 7.
Telephone (+353 1) 679 2169
Fax (+353 1) 677 2328

ISBN 0-9538125-0-2

Text is typeset in 13 point Perpetua with captions in 11 point.

Origination
Layout and design by Declan Clancy

Typesetting and page formatting from authors' discs, all photos and line drawings
scanned and placed by
Typeform Repro, Portside Business Centre, East Wall Road, Dublin 3.
Telephone 855 3855.

Film output, printing and binding
ColourBooks Ltd, 105 Baldoyle Industrial Estate, Dublin 13. Telephone 832 5812.

Dedicated to
the Young Sailors
of Ireland

Contents

Foreword

The story of the development of Ireland's sail training scheme is both fascinating and heart-warming, and it is told here for the first time by Eric Healy, whose preparation of the original manuscript was a labour of love, and by W.M. Nixon, who has a deep interest in the scheme. Between them they have produced an excellent book which, while impressive in its detail, is written in an easy style that will make it attractive not only to the many thousands who have sailed on our sail training vessels over the years, but also to anyone with an interest in sailing ships.

Michael Smith TD
Minister for Defence
Chairman of *Coiste an Asgard*

It is fitting that this book should re-tell the story of *Asgard*, the small ketch that played such an important role in the history of our nation and, much later, served as our first sail training vessel. I am proud to be associated with the plans which are now in train to restore *Asgard* to full sailing and seaworthy condition.

Today, we have in the handsome brigantine *Asgard II*, one of the world's most successful sail training ships. She is very unusual among government training ships in that trainee berths on her are open to all young people between the ages of 16 and 25. You do no need any special qualifications or experience to enjoy the benefits of sailing on *Asgard II*. All that is required is a young person's interest in seeing the world through the medium of traditional sail on a Tall Ship, and, aboard *Asgard II*, that world can become your oyster.

Over the years *Asgard II* has become a very special informal maritime ambassador for all the people of Ireland. She acts, too, as a wonderful focal point for Irish people in distant lands. With the very favourable impression she makes in foreign ports and among the sail training vessels of other nations, there is a growing enthusiasm among the international fleet of Tall Ships for visits to Ireland.

The way that this brought about the impressive Tall Ships Parades in Cork and Belfast in 1991, and more recently the memorable Tall Ships "invasion" of Dublin in 1998, is recounted in this book in colourful detail. Such great events do not happen without an enormous amount of voluntary organisational effort and enthusiasm by very many people who share a passionate belief in the profound value of sail training.

The same voluntary enthusiasm and effort have also been the basis of *Coiste an Asgard,* whose members have given freely of their time and their vast collective experience of maritime matters and sound management, in order to ensure that our sail training programme is efficiently and effectively run to provide the best possible service for our young people.

I take this opportunity to pay tribute to all those who have served as members of *An Coiste* over the years and have created a situation whereby Ireland has a developing sail training programme appropriate to the needs of the 21st Century.

We owe them our heartfelt thanks.

Michael Smith

Michael Smith T.D.
Minister for Defence.
April 2000

Board of Directors of *Coiste an Asgard*

Chairman:	Michael Smith TD, Minister for Defence

John Boland

Manus Brennan

David Byrne

Madlin Curran

Sean Flood*

Avril Harris

Patrick Hogan

Commodore John Kavanagh

Clayton Love Jnr

Mr Justice Frederick Morris

Enda O'Coineen

Gerard O'Donnell

Patrick J O'Hara

William O'Mahony

*National representative on Committee of International Sail Training Association.

Authors' Acknowledgements

We have been greatly encouraged by the view of those in Irish sail training that this is a book which has been long needed. Its authors readily acknowledge that it has been very long in its gestation. But the story it tells is no ordinary tale.

Captain Eric Healy would particularly like to record his thanks to his sister Ruth Heard, and to Jeremy Addis, for their assistance in preparing his original manuscript in order to present the concept of a book about Irish sail training to *Coiste an Asgard.*

Both authors wish to acknowledge the enthusiastic support of the members of *Coiste an Asgard* in their steadfast encouragement of the vision of expanding the story of Irish sail training in order to set it in its historical context, and show how it has developed to meet the needs of the 21st Century. In the latter context, we have been particularly assisted by the perceptive thoughts of Captain Tom McCarthy and Captain Rohan MacAllister.

Everyone involved in this project is in turn grateful to Richard Burrows and his colleagues at Irish Distillers for their sponsorship support through John Power & Son. The success of the products of Irish Distillers is ultimately reliant on the correct period of maturation, and we hope that this book will reflect the same process.

The production, printing and finishing of a one-off book of this nature is something of a team effort, yet each member of the team has to be possessed of exceptional individual talent and dedication. It simply would not have happened without the very special input of Declan Clancy, whose enthusiasm for book production is a joy to behold.

Declan in his turn received support way above the call of duty from Robert Healy and Pat Conneely at Typeform Repro, and John Harold and Adrienne Foran of ColourBooks. We are grateful to all of them, and to Betty Clancy for generously allowing her home to be used as a production facility.

The boat plans are the work of Michael Tyrrell and Myles Stapleton, and we know that their very special skills have added greatly to the quality and technical interest of the book. We also wish to extend special thanks to Christine Hayden of the *Asgard* Office for her assistance, particularly in the final hectic stages of book production.

The fact that we have been able to include nearly 240 illustrations from very many sources is indicative, we hope, of the book's value as a record of an important part of Ireland's maritime history. The enthusiastic response of photographers and the owners of important photographs has reinforced this hope.

Those involved in sourcing, supplying, or taking the photographs include Des Barrington, David Beattie, Gabriel Bradley, David Branigan, Brendan Connor, Tom Cronin, Ted Crosbie, Kevin Dwyer, Ciaran Earley, Mark Fitzell, John Fitzpatrick, Sean Flood, Brendan Fogarty, Captain Bennie Forde, Daphne French, Tom Furlong, Louise Gunn, Theo Harris, Christine Hayden, Ron Jones, Pat Langan, Frank Larkin, Tom Lawlor, Niall Leahy, Rohan MacAllister, Grant McEwen, Kevin MacLaverty, Sean McLaughlin, Ursula Maguire, Max Mudie, Brian Nixon, David O'Brien, Enda O'Coineen, Paddy O'Hara, Padraic O'Reilly, Sean Patterson, Willie Richardson, Charles Sargent, William Stokes, Pat Sweeney, Brian Tucker, John Tynan, Michael Tyrrell and Harry Whelehan.

They all have our heartfelt thanks, and we sincerely apologise to anyone who has been inadvertently omitted from this list.

At a personal level, Eric Healy would like to give special thanks to those enthusiasts who gave freely of their own time in the *Asgard* Maintenance Weekends in the early days of Irish sail training, for their help was both practical and encouraging.

And W.M.Nixon would especially like to thank Managing Editor David O'Brien and his colleagues in *Afloat* Magazine for their generous tolerance of their Contributing Editor's re-direction of his energies during the accelerating production of this book, and to Georgina Campbell Nixon of GCG Guides Ltd for showing the same kind forbearance.

W.M.Nixon and Captain Eric Healy
February 2000

1 The timeless power of sail

Modern commercial shipping functions with minimal crew numbers, and today's technology makes the notion of totally unmanned sea-going freighters an attainable concept. Yet in many countries with maritime interests, an alternative vision of seagoing is increasingly significant. In it, the ideal is towards the most labour-intensive vessels possible. These sailing ships rely on ancient skills and traditional equipment to harness the wind's power, thereby giving their crews a more profound experience of seafaring. The physical teamwork involved provides a deeper insight into inter-personal working relationships, with the encouragement of character development. This is the world of international sail training.

For seafarers imbued with the great traditions of sail, the inexorable changeover to powered ships during the 19th and 20th Centuries was a long and painful experience. The sea is an unforgiving place, and sailors are by nature conservative. It has been rightly observed that while there are old sailors, and there are bold sailors, there are no old bold sailors. Inevitably, however, commercial interest dictated the agenda and the pace of change. Gradually, the improvement of steam and then diesel power, and their greater reliability in terms of time-keeping, saw sail in retreat.

One of the first steamships to be seen in Ireland was the 80ft paddle-driven *Thames,* built in Glasgow in 1815 by the engineer John Dodd. He made a

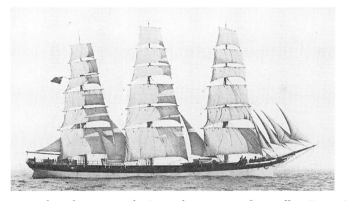

Commercial sail was never so handsome as in its dying days, as is elegantly demonstrated by the full rigged ship *Largiemore* on her first sail in 1892. Between 1888 and 1893, there was an international "windjammer boom" in shipbuilding, and one of the firms which contributed most was the Scottish company of Russell & Co on the Clyde. In the four years 1890 to 1893, this one yard's *annual* output of big steel sailing ships "was nearer 30 than 20 vessels". One of the finest of them was the 1938-ton 263ft *Largiemore,* which could carry a cargo of 3,300 tons. She was built in 1892 for the northern Irish firm of Thomson, Dickie & Co, which owned her until 1910.

promotional voyage with this revolutionary vessel from Scotland to London with calls at Dublin, Wexford and southwest Wales before rounding Land's End and visiting the naval port of Plymouth, where senior officers famously gave the opinion that, some day in the distant future, steam ships might be useful for towing their great sailing warships out of port. Within a few years, steam vessels of up to a hundred tons were to be found providing a limited alternative service on the main cross channel routes between the Dublin area and Holyhead in North Wales. But the continuing hold which sail had on traditional seafarers was remarkable.

For something which had formerly been so useful to mankind in the exploration and commercial development of the world was not going to be abandoned lightly. And sail was never more spectacular than in its dying days. The great sailing ships of the late 19th century came to be seen as the very epitome of beauty. Any seaman who had run through the Great Southern Ocean and rounded Cape Horn under square rig was someone meriting special veneration and respect. And long after steam was in the ascendant, it was thought essential to have trained in sail before you could qualify as a fully-competent ship's officer on a steamship.

The dogged persistence of commercial sail for years after mechanical power had proven its value is put into focus by an analysis of activity at the little port of Skerries on the Fingal coast north of Dublin. Then, as now, the development of passenger vessels more readily utilised new technology, and the first steamship seen in Skerries was the 22-ton *Queen*, which carried passengers on a day trip from Dublin in 1887.

The soaring beauty of sail in the late 19th Century – the tea clipper *Cutty Sark,* built in 1869, was a global style-setter for both deep sea and coastal vessels.

While this was all of seventy-two years after the first steamer had been in Dublin, at the time more than ninety small sailing ships were discharging and loading cargoes at Skerries pier every year. It wasn't until 1900 that the first steam vessel discharged a cargo of coal at Skerries. By that time, both Skerries and sail were in decline, and by 1914, only twenty-eight cargo vessels used the port, with ten of them steamers. By the 1930s, steam itself was being challenged by diesel power, such that it wasn't unknown to hear sailors of the old school talking of their ships as being "driven by steam as nature intended". Thus in 1934 we find that only fourteen cargo vessels used Skerries harbour – five sailing schooners (some with auxiliary power), three steamships, and six motor vessels.

By the late 1940s, commercial sail had disappeared completely from Skerries, and in 1954 the port was used only by three steam vessels and five motor ships. In 1961, Skerries had its final year as a cargo port, with just three motor vessels discharging coal. In view of the nature of those last cargoes, it was ironic that steam had gone the way of sail. Yet romantic and all as the finest steamships may have been, there was no discernible movement in favour of steamship training as part of a proper seafaring background. But although sail had been totally eclipsed as a means of commercial transport, there was a persistent movement in favour of sail as an important part of sea training.

Today, a number of countries still use experience under sail as an integral part of their professional mariners' training. Several navies pride themselves on the elegant style of their large sail training vessels – academy ships – which are seen as imbuing their crews with a tangible sense of their nation's maritime history, while providing an awareness of the more traditional ship-handling skills. These special vessels also act as very effective maritime ambassadors in ports around the world, notable examples being the Italy's three masted ship *Amerigo Vespucci,* and the US Coastguard Academy's handsome barque *Eagle.*

But the newer idea that experiencing seafaring under sail is in itself something intrinsically useful, regardless of whether or not the young trainee hopes to go on to a career at sea, or indeed ever sails again at all, is in many ways the most interesting of all the many notions which have developed from the concept of sail training. As life becomes ever more specialised, and as we lead existences increasingly sheltered from nature's reality, the sheer breadth of experience which is provided by sailing the sea in a traditionally rigged vessel, and the heightened sense of interpersonal working relationships which comes with it, together with the broader vision of the world which can be given to people from every sort of background, makes it something of special value in national and international life.

The development of this contemporary style of sail training in Ireland inevitably reflects our complex history. There is, for instance, a line of thought which maintains that Ireland has never been a truly maritime nation. This may stem from the mistaken expectation that being an island should lead naturally to the development of very strong seafaring traditions. Yet if we look at the most determinedly maritime regions of history, we find that, far from being islands, they tend rather to be coastal regions on the edges either of large and powerful countries, or peripheral to areas of economically vigorous or at least over-crowded populations. An outstanding example is the Phoenicians of the eastern Mediterranean. And in Europe, three classic cases in point are Galicia in northwest Spain, Brittany on France's western seaboard, and the peninsula of Devon and Cornwall thrusting into the Atlantic to the southwest of the English mainland.

The Basque people, too, crowded into their small area in northern Spain and southwest France, have long looked to the sea for their economic salvation,

A modern academy ship – Poland's *Dar Mlodziezy* ("Gift of Youth"), seen here getting under way in Cork Harbour during the Tall Ships visit in 1991, was built in 1984 at Gdansk. She is 108 metres (358ft) in overall length, and carries 33 professional crew, 181 cadets, and 20 "paying sail trainees".

5

The Portuguese caravels were the ocean-ranging flagships of a determinedly maritime small nation state. They set lateen rigged sails, which gave a windward performance significantly better than that provided by square rig

but not as a means to conquest. Thus the Genoese explorer John Sebastian Cabot, in his "discovery" of Newfoundland in 1497 on behalf of the merchant adventurers of Bristol, reported that the cod-rich seas in the area were being fished by hundreds of Basque vessels, and the indications are that the hardy Basques had been active for many years in what were to become the "new" American fisheries. Those other even earlier discoverers of North America, the Vikings, were to some extent also thrust into a strong maritime awareness from their heartlands in the Scandinavian peninsulas by pressures of population. But perhaps the most telling example of all is to be found in the great voyages of Portugal, the first identifiable European maritime nation state. The governmental encouragement of the Portuguese sea explorers was surely motivated to a considerable extent by that little nation's precarious location on the edge of Spain.

By contrast, the early settlers in Ireland had no need for extensive voyaging offshore, for their fertile land was uncrowded. Even as an Irish nation emerged, it inhabited a land flowing in milk and honey in which cattle were infinitely more important than the fish of the sea. And of course there was no way that Celtic Ireland was in any way an organised nation state in the subsequent manner of Portugal and England in the late Middle Ages. Yet at the time when Ireland was the island of saints and scholars, some remarkable seafaring by individuals rather than organised groups was being achieved. Thus while the Irish may not have been a maritime nation, some of them were most certainly a seafaring people. And their great seafarers had the very special distinction of going to sea for spiritual reasons, rather than conquest or commercial gain.

The explorer Tim Severin demonstrated in 1976 that the possibly mythical transoceanic voyages of St Brendan the Navigator were well within the realms of possibility. And it is a fact that as the Vikings spread out in the 8th Century across the islands of the North Atlantic towards Iceland, and later Greenland and North America, they found Irish monastic settlements already established in remote archipelagos. For instance, the best harbour in the Faeroe Islands —

Sea trials off the Kerry coast in 1976 for Tim Severin's re-creation of a large currach.
He used this frail vessel to demonstrate that the legends of the voyages of St Brendan the
Navigator could have been based on historical fact.

the inlet of Vestmanna on the island of Streymoy – was so named by the Vikings because it was already the home port of the "Western Men" – the Irish.

By the time the precursors of the modern nation state were coming into being, the Celtic peoples voyaged about the seas of far western Europe with relative freedom. Thus Scotland was named for the people of the Scoti tribe who settled the Hebrides and Highlands from northwest Ireland. This seaborne interlinking of the isles on the Celtic fringe was re-lived when a noted modern sailor, Wallace Clark, re-created in 1963 the voyage of St Columba in 563 from Derry to Iona. Further to explore the realities of the regular seafaring on the Celtic fringe, in 1993 Wallace Clark had the *Aileach,* a reproduction early mediaeval sailing galley, built in Donegal. The *Aileach* voyaged between the west of Ireland and the Hebrides, and subsequently further north to the Faeroes.

But it wasn't only to the northern and western seas that Ireland's maritime links were forged. It has been said, with as much truth as wit, that the Irish are a Mediterranean people left out in the rain. Certainly in the best traditions of the western Mediterranean languages, the Irish words for sea and mother stem from the same linguistic root, which is not the case in the Germanic languages.

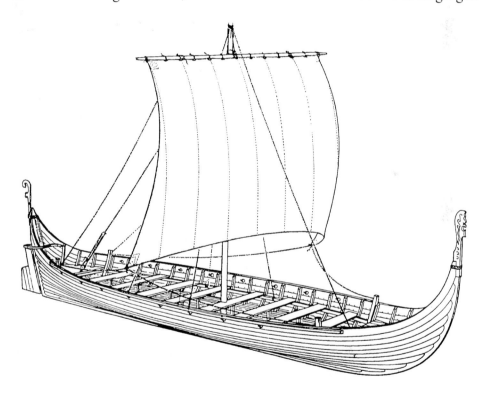

The *Aileach,* Wallace Clark's reproduction of a Western Isles Galley of Mediaeval times, was built in Donegal in 1993, and sailed between the west of Ireland and the Hebrides. She subsequently voyaged to the Faeroes.

This suggests a more complex yet comfortable relationship with the sea. And always, there was this tradition of regular seaborn communication between Ireland, Cornwall, Brittany and northwest Spain. These sea routes were taken by the missionaries going forth from Ireland in the Dark Ages to bring Christianity back to Europe, and as more settled times returned, a regular route was established across the Bay of Biscay for the great pilgrimages to Santiago de Compostela in Galicia. St James's Gate in Dublin, today the home of the Guinness brewery, is so named because it was here that the pilgrims of Santiago – St James – traditionally gathered before beginning their journey and voyaging from Ireland to northwest Spain

At a more prosaic level, we have only to look at surnames frequently occurring in modern Ireland to realise that, before the English conquests, seafaring was an important part of Irish life. The second most common Irish surname of Murphy – *O Morchoe* – means "Sea Hound". And anyone called Doyle is descended from the Vikings, with the sea in his veins. Admittedly it could be argued that, in both cases, the only certainty is that a distant ancestor came in from the sea. But nevertheless it seems reasonable to suggest that it wasn't so much that Ireland was never a maritime nation, as that maritime Ireland was never a nation in the modern sense.

By contrast, the English had their own sense of rapidly developing nationality interwoven with the fact of becoming a great sea power, and it was central to their vision of themselves as they swept over Ireland in the late Middle Ages. History is written by the victors, and it suited these conquerors that any home grown Irish maritime tradition should be obliterated. At a more practical level, those self-same merchant venturers of Bristol who were to send Cabot to Newfoundland in 1497 had since 1171 been allocated mastery of the port of Dublin, and they had long expected that their reward from the conquest of Ireland would be a monopoly of all trade routes. So all native Irish merchant shipping of any significance was ruthlessly suppressed.

Then, as the English commercial expansion and conquest developed into the concept of the British Empire, any small remaining Irish maritime tradition was subsumed into the great new adventure of "Britishness". But Ireland's involvement was only as a very junior partner. As recently as 1805, Nelson's famous signal at Trafalgar was: "England expects that every man will do his duty". Notwithstanding the Acts of Union with Scotland in 1707 and with Ireland in 1801, the expectations and sense of identity of the Scots and the Irish, not to mention the Welsh in the oldest colony of all, were of little account at the centre of power in England. Even when the British Empire was already showing signs of decline in the 20th century, this Anglocentric attitude was never far below the surface, and it was well illustrated by the explorer Robert Scott – "Scott of the Antarctic" – in his valedictory note in January 1912. "Had we lived" wrote Scott, "I should have had a tale to tell of hardihood, endurance and courage of my companions, which would have stirred the heart of every Englishman ..."

Despite everything which that underlying attitude suggests, as the British Empire came to full vigour during the 19th Century, it developed enough affluence to spread increased economic vitality even to the remotest corners of all four nations then within Britain. Notwithstanding the ill-effects of the famine of 1845-49, locally-owned shipping became an expanding feature of Irish commercial life, and to some extent it is the nostalgic old sepia-tinted photos from the 1880s and 1890s of Irish harbours well filled with each port's own schooners and trading ketches which today colour our romantic view of what a proper sail training vessel should be like.

In fact, the reality was more prosaic. To put it in perspective, the little locally-owned trading schooners sailing from Irish ports large and small were the equivalent, in their time, of the juggernaut trucks which today set forth from all our cities, towns and villages to criss-cross Ireland and Europe carrying goods of all kinds to the most distant parts. It was a harsh life then, and today's trucker has a hard time of it too. The romance of travel has little to do with it, just as the romance of sail had little to do with it in the old days of the schooners. But as the commercial reality of expanding steamship numbers intruded more forcefully with every passing year, in Ireland as elsewhere the traditions of sail had their devoted adherents.

In the Irish context, the growth of mechanised power was to have a political resonance, as Belfast rapidly developed into one of the world's greatest centres of steamship construction. But even in the more gently moving south of Ireland, the new way of things was making itself felt. As long ago as 1865, a 685-ton iron steamship, the *Kiushiu Maru,* was built on the shores of Cork Harbour for the Mitsu Bishi Company of Yokohama in Japan. However, over on

Dungarvan in County Waterford was a successful Irish schooner port in the late 19th Century, with several locally-owned craft, of which one of the best known was the *Village Girl* (centre). Scenes such as this typify the romantic image of sail. Yet the sails are unfurled in picturesque style simply because, before the invention of synthetic sailcloth, the expensive sails had to be dried whenever possible to prevent rot. And while these are handsome little vessels, in purely economic terms they were really only the equivalent of today's juggernaut trucks.

Ireland's East Coast, the river port of Arklow, originally founded as a Viking trading settlement, was to continue as a stronghold of sail, famous for its commercially viable trading schooners until well into the 20th Century.

By that time, Ireland had been through much turmoil with the War of Independence and the Civil War. When the newly established Irish Free State came into existence in 1922, it was a particularly traumatic experience for those involved with the maritime world. The essence of the British Empire lay in sea power in its most vigorous expression, and any Irish professional seafarer with qualifications would most probably have obtained them in England, as there were very few nautical teaching institutions in Ireland.

Admittedly, some of those who experienced it have been known to recall that sending any sensitive and lonely Irish youth – of whatever background – to spend his most formative years in an emphatically English educational establishment could sometimes result in the creation of an Irish Republican of unexpected intensity. Nevertheless, the maritime establishment in Ireland, which had manifested itself through the Royal Navy, the Merchant Marine, Irish Lights, and the Lifeboat Institute as well as recreational boating of all kinds, had a strongly British tinge and Unionist bias, so there was a natural antipathy and feeling of mistrust between it and the new state.

Yet it was Irish recreational sailing, that very yachting which had been so much a part of the old Ascendancy's way of life, which was to provide the most vivid expression of the new state's maritime identity. When Conor O'Brien sailed around the world south of the great capes between 1923 and 1925 in the relatively small 42ft ketch *Saoirse,* he was not only pioneering a route never before sailed by a small cruising yacht, but he was also making the first major voyage to be undertaken by any vessel registered in the Irish Free State and flying the tricolour as her ensign. And the gallant little *Saoirse* – which translates as "Freedom" and was named in honour of the new state – was a product of one of the few nautical training establishments actually located in Ireland, as she was built in West Cork in 1922 by Tom Moynihan and his shipwrights in the boatyard attached to the Fisheries School in Baltimore.

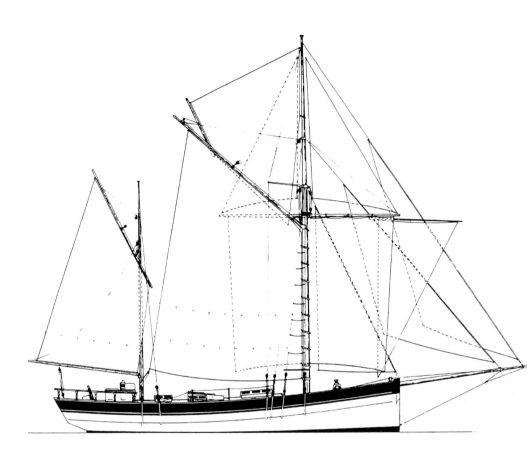

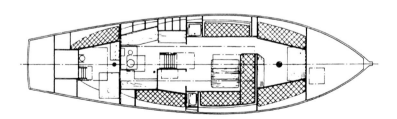

Saoirse was built in Baltimore, West Cork, in 1922

Conor O'Brien (1860-1952) — patriot, sailor, mountaineer, architect and author — had already entered the national consciousness with his involvement with Erskine Childers and the gun-running of 1914, which we detail in the next chapter. But in 1923-25 he entered global maritime awareness with this extraordinary voyage in a little ship which he'd designed himself, although he asserted that her hull shape was actually based on an

Conor O'Brien.

Arklow fishing boat of the 1860s, forging yet another link in that East Coast port's pivotal role in Irish voyaging under sail.

However, although *Saoirse* may have been built in a nautical training establishment, her voyage round the world was often far from being a good example of sail training at its best, as O'Brien tended to set unattainably high standards for his mostly amateur shipmates, and he was notorious for his short temper. Thus he had so many crew changes that it's reckoned eighteen different people were involved in *Saoirse's* great voyage. Nevertheless there was one interesting example of the way that "sail training", in its broadest sense, could be mutually beneficial for a ship's company. In the South Pacific, by now desperate to recruit crew, O'Brien signed on a young Tongan car mechanic and taxi driver called Kioa who had voyaged to distant places in a variety of craft, but was reputed to be something of a ne'er-do-well ashore. In the light of the subsequent international experience of sail training, we should not be surprised that in Kioa, *Saoirse* found her most enthusiastic and effective crewman, and he was still aboard and on good terms with O'Brien when the great voyage finished in Dun Laoghaire at 1630 hrs on June 20th 1925, having started at precisely 1630 hrs on June 20th 1923.

Conor O'Brien had further experience of useful deep sea training under sail the year after the *Saoirse* voyage finished when, in the latter half of 1926, he made the 8,000 mile passage out to the Falkland Islands in the new 56ft auxiliary ketch *Ilen*. This interesting craft had been designed by O'Brien and built in Baltimore to be the service vessel for the Falkland Islands Company as a

The 56ft ketch *Ilen* sailing in Dublin Bay, May 1998. She was brought back from the Falklands to Ireland under an initiative led by Gary MacMahon of Limerick.

result of the favourable impression which *Saoirse* had made on the professional seamen working in the islands when she sailed into Port Stanley after rounding Cape Horn in December 1924.

To crew for him on this delivery voyage, O'Brien had two cousins from Cape Clear, Denis and Con Cadogan, who were keen to gain deep sea time in working towards professional ship's officer qualifications. In those days, experience under sail was still very highly regarded, so the *Ilen* offered 'The Capers' a golden opportunity. Thus it was a purposeful, successful and pleasant voyage, with a happy outcome of almost fairytale proportions to conclude the story in what was then the distant future. For although the gallant little *Saoirse* was to be lost at her moorings during a hurricane in Jamaica in 1979, *Ilen* continued about her work in the Falklands until the 1990s, and then she was shipped home to Ireland in November 1997 for honourable retirement in Limerick City, Conor O'Brien having come from Limerick county.

By the time of *Ilen's* return in the late 1990s, much had happened in Irish maritime life and sail training. While *Saoirse's* voyage may have been an inspiration for the 1920s, the "Economic War" of the 1930s provided an unhappy time for Irish seafarers, and especially those who remained enthusiastic about sailing ships. Sail may have been in decline as a commercial force, but its full romance was still being stylishly expressed by the Scandinavian square riggers, notably those owned by the legendary Captain Eriksson at his Baltic base in the Aland Islands between Sweden and Finland.

Eriksson's Tall Ships carried cadets both as crew and for sail training purposes in the ultimate seafaring university of Cape Horn. His mighty vessels visited Cork and Dublin from time to time, their graceful presence, evocative of the call of the high seas, providing painful reminders of the way that Ireland was receding from the maritime world. However, not everyone accepted that it was totally a lost cause. In the Autumn of 1935, Eriksson's mighty full-rigged ship *Pamir* was in Dublin port. She was one of the German-built "Flying Ps", a sister ship of the *Padua* which, as the *Kruzenshtern,* was herself to visit Dublin with the Tall Ships Fleet in 1998.

The call of the high seas. The *Pamir* airs her sails in Dublin, Autumn 1935

"The irresistible silent march of the great ship under 50,000 square feet of canvas....."
A photograph by Daphne French aboard the *Pamir* on the voyage to Australia.

Back in 1935, visions of a fleet of square rigged ships in the Liffey seemed beyond the wildest dreams. The assumption was that the great sailing ships were a doomed species, so anyone who wanted to experience sailing on them had to grasp any opportunity that was offered. The young Irish sailing enthusiast Daphne French, a niece of the songwriter Percy French, contrived with her friend Betty Parsons to get signed on as Stewardesses aboard the *Pamir* at the pay rate of one shilling per month for the voyage out to Australia.

The outward passage to the Spencer Gulf in southern Australia was made in ballast. French wrote of it: "The irresistible silent march of the great ship, under 50,000 square feet of canvas, was a fine sensation. She did not roll much, even in very light weather. Her greatest angle of heel, in a sudden tropical squall, was 33 degrees".

But the long voyage was no joyride for the two Irish girls, as feeding the afterguard became increasingly difficult with the inevitable deterioration of stores – "one occasionally found a maggot in the porridge, but the Captain said 'it gave body to it'…" Aboard the ship, the girls were regarded as bringers of luck, as they got to Port Lincoln from Dublin in 77 days, a record for the *Pamir*.

They returned to Europe around Cape Horn, again as Stewardesses, but this time aboard another Eriksson ship, *l'Avenir,* which made a good passage,

L'Avenir brought Daphne French back from Australia in 1936

despite being heavily laden with grain, to reach Falmouth in England in 95 days. "We didn't see the Horn, being as far south as 57 degrees, but the sun was shining and the sea was as quiet as a Scottish loch." However, at other stages of the voyage they experienced genuinely heavy weather, yet neither – to their delight – was seasick. Their straight-forward pleasure in their experience shines down the years like a bright light amid the pervading gloom of the 1930s.

Ireland's declaration of neutrality at the outbreak of World War II in 1939 provided seafarers and the maritime movement with even greater problems. Irish Shipping Ltd had to be created in emergency conditions in order to carry cargoes of vital supplies to an isolated nation, and in order to train officers for the fledgling company, considerable demands were put on the Irish Nautical College, a one-room establishment on the Dublin quays under the direction of Captain Tom Walsh.

Originally founded as the Dublin School of Navigation and Seamanship in 1889, the needs of wartime had led to the revival of an almost defunct organisation under its new name. The authorities needed a Principal to head the rejuvenated College, and Tom Walsh had shown interest in the job. But he was not fully qualified for the task, even with an Extra Master's Certificate. The problem was solved by sending him in command of one of Irish Shipping's vessels on a winter Transatlantic wartime voyage to Canada, and as a fully fledged Master Mariner, Tom Walsh then took over the direction of the Irish Nautical College to begin many years of service in the training of seafarers.

While Tom Walsh's great work was as a teacher of steamship officers and crew, his little college also had an interesting sideline assessing and issuing Yachtmaster's Certificates to Irish sailing enthusiasts who hoped to serve the Allied cause in the war by availing of the Royal Naval Volunteer Reserve's willingness to offer commissions to appropriately experienced sailing enthusiasts. Interviews for the RNVR were primarily based on the interviewee's sailing ability and experience, but this was combined with a consideration of educational qualifications. Amongst Irish sailing enthusiasts who were interested in joining the RNVR, the reckoning was that having a Yachtmaster's Certificate was beneficial, even if it had little to do with sailing. For until 1970 it

A natural teacher – Captain Tom Walsh lecturing at the Nautical College in Dun Laoghaire in December 1957.

21

The Arklow sailing trader *Lady of Avenel,* aboard which Jack Tyrrell sailed as a schoolboy. Although usually referred to as "one of the Arklow schooners", at the time this owner's picture was painted in traditional style she was rigged as a brigantine.

was almost the same as the Foreign Master's ticket, though with some subjects left out of a syllabus which didn't include sail training at all.

After the war, the Nautical College was re-located in 1950 to Dun Laoghaire Harbour. In 1954, Tom Walsh found that his friend Jack Tyrrell of Arklow had come up with the most beautiful idea. Although he had been running the successful family boat-building business in Arklow since 1924, both as manager and in-house naval architect, Jack Tyrrell's fondest memories were of his school holidays when he had sailed as a very junior crewman aboard his uncle's Arklow trading schooner, the *Lady of Avenel.* Ever since, he had remained convinced that a period of sail training was beneficial for any seaman even if he spent all his working life in steam or diesel, and so in 1954 he sketched out the plans of a 110ft sail training barquentine "for Cadets to the Irish Merchant Service".

By any standards, this proposed three-masted vessel setting squaresails on her foremast was a strikingly handsome ship. Even in countries where sail training was part of the national maritime ethos, few vessels could have matched her looks. But she was the beauty that never was. In the Ireland of the 1950s, she was an idea both ahead of its time, yet also behind the times. For at a period of only slowly increasing prosperity, sail training of merchant marine cadets was an idea fading under the baleful examination of accountants. And the notion of sail training as a useful experience to offset the pressures of modern life was an idea only in its infancy.

A glimpse of what was then the future. The crew aloft as the Portuguese sail training ship *Sagres* is towed out of the River Dart in the south of England before the start of the first "modern" sail training race, from Torbay to Lisbon in 1956.

23

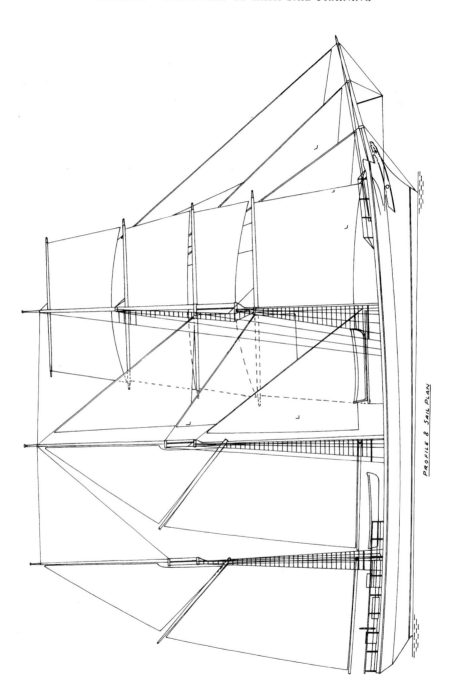

PROFILE & SAIL PLAN

Jack Tyrrell's 1954 proposals for a 110ft sail training barquentine.

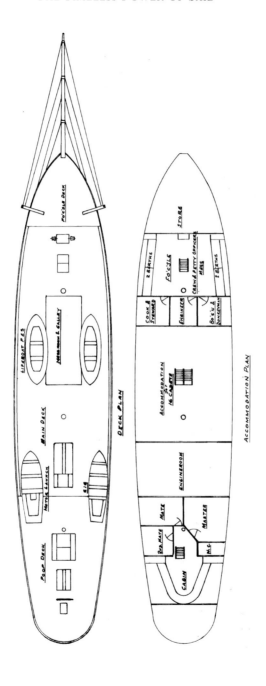

DECK PLAN

ACCOMMODATION PLAN

Yet it was an idea coming slowly to maturity, while the more traditional concept of sail training and Tall Ships as an integral part of the official life of a maritime nation continued to prosper in several countries. In 1956, the first modern sail training race, from Torbay across the Bay of Biscay to Lisbon, took place, and from it there emerged the Sail Training Association and ultimately the International Sail Training Association. That first race of 1956 was a remarkable amalgam of traditional sail training for professional seafarers and naval cadets as exemplified by the great square riggers, and smaller craft representing the new movement for providing seagoing experience for anyone who wanted it.

Ireland was not represented, other than by a very few individual crewmen on vessels from other countries. But only five years later, in 1961, the 51ft ketch *Asgard* was brought home to Ireland, and the long and sometimes painful process of developing a national sail training movement could begin.

2   A ship of the gods

The building of Erskine Childers' *Asgard*, and her history 1905-1968

The inspiration, conception and construction of the 51ft ketch *Asgard*, and her voyaging and exploits between 1905 and 1914, involved a remarkable selection of able and talented people. Their achievements with this fine ship were exceptional in their scope and variety. And the consequences of their actions and adventures have a significance which continues to resonate down the ages on both sea and land.

Asgard was designed and built by Colin Archer of Larvik in Norway in 1905. He was of Scottish descent, his father having migrated across the North Sea from Newburgh by the Firth of Tay on Scotland's East Coast. However, throughout

Colin Archer aged 73 in 1905, when he designed and built *Asgard* for Erskine and Molly Childers. Coincidentally, Jack Tyrrell of Arklow was also 73 when, in 1973, he produced the preliminary drawings for *Asgard II*.

Typical of Colin Archer's *Redningskoites* was the *Svolvaer*, seen here from one of her sister-ships while manoeuvring in close company.

his long life from 1832 to 1921, Colin Archer was to play a role of increasing national and international importance in Norwegian life as his family's new homeland re-established its own identity and sought peaceful separation from Sweden.

His special contribution lay in his skills as a marine architect and master shipwright, a vital role as Norway's maritime expertise was central to the country's economic well-being and sense of purpose. Thus not only did Archer design and build Nansen's famous Arctic exploration vessel *Fram,* but as well his boatyard at Tolderodden on a promontory in the small town of Larvik near the approaches to Oslo was to see the development and building of the *Redningskoites,* rugged sailing lifeboats whose design was evolved by Archer to cope with the tough conditions of the Norwegian west coast.

But he also realised the significance, in this growing Norwegian maritime awareness, of using the sea for recreational purposes. He was an early member of what was to become the Royal Norwegian Yacht Club, and his boatyard became a place of pilgrimage for determined yachtsmen who sought craft which could confidently keep the sea in rough conditions, and yet perform well when the winds were gentle. Archer's skill in developing such vessels amounted to genius. Although he was already 73 in 1905 when he designed and built *Asgard,* he was at the height of his powers as a yacht designer, and the new boat was one of the finest seaworthy cruising yachts of her day.

In view of *Asgard's* subsequent history, it is a poignant irony to note that 1905 was the year in which Norwegian independence became peacefully complete. But while *Asgard* has great significance through her role in Irish national history, and in Irish sail training, we must never forget that she is of special value in herself, a splendid example of all that was best in seagoing yacht design in 1905.

She was built as a wedding present for a young Anglo-Irishman, Robert Erskine Childers (1870-1922), and his American bride, Mary "Molly" Osgood of Boston. Childers was only six when he lost his father, the noted English Oriental scholar Robert Caesar Childers, to tuberculosis. Though his mother was to survive for another eight years before she succumbed to the same disease, with his father's death Childers and his four siblings effectively became orphans, raised by his mother's family, the Bartons of Glendalough House at Annamoe in County Wicklow.

Thus although he was educated through the classic English public school and university system, all childhood holidays were spent in Wicklow, where his deepening love for Ireland was matched by his growing enthusiasm for the outdoor life. In his early twenties, he re-activated a boyhood interest in boats, and he and his brother made their first cruise – to Scotland from Dublin Bay – in 1893 when he was still 22.

In 1894, after graduating from Cambridge, he began his career as a Clerk in the House of Commons in London, and had thoughts of eventually becoming a Member of Parliament. His activities afloat continued in the waters of the Thames Estuary, the North Sea, and the English Channel, and he began to contribute articles to sailing magazines, as well as becoming an active member of the Cruising Club, which had been formed in London in 1880 to cater for the needs of seagoing non-racers, and did this so successfully that in 1902 it was to become the Royal Cruising Club.

In the late Summer and Autumn of 1897, Childers made an extensive cruise among the islands of the North Sea coasts of The Netherlands and Germany, and then went on through the Kiel Canal to Denmark. His experiences were to give him the germ of an idea for a book. But meanwhile, from March to September 1900, he served in South Africa in the Boer War with a sub-division of the Honourable Artillery Company. His experiences there planted in him the first tiny doubts about the morality of the British Imperial mission. Nevertheless an "instant book" on the Boer War, assembled from his highly readable letters home, proved a popular patriotic seller.

Back in London, he resumed writing the book inspired by his 1897 cruise. When it was published in 1903, *The Riddle of the Sands* was an immediate success, and it has never been out of print since, having sold more than two million copies. It is both a thriller, and a very accurate and entertaining portrayal of small boat cruising. The two heroes, Davies and Carruthers in their little yawl *Dulcibella*, stumble on the fact that the Kaiser's government in Germany is secretly building a fleet of barges for an invasion of Britain across the North Sea from the hidden harbours among those sandy islands and waterways which Childers had cruised in 1897.

The Riddle of the Sands struck many chords, and it has been given part of the credit for the Royal Navy's expansion of its North Sea fleet in the lead-up to World War I, and the development of a new naval base at Rosyth on Scotland's East Coast. So true to life was its narrative that, many years later, people still assumed it was basically factual, and that the *Dulcibella* had been a real boat. She had indeed been based to a considerable extent on the *Vixen,* with which Childers' 1897 cruise had been made, but she and *The Riddle of the Sands* were fictional. Nevertheless, some seventy years after *The Riddle* was first published, the skipper of the *Asgard* was to receive serious enquiries requesting copies of the hull lines and sail plan of *Dulcibella.*

But even as the book's wide readership and vivid portrayal of German plans were focusing English minds to the eastward, its busy author was ever more preoccupied with the situation to the west, both in his second home in Ireland, and in America. In the Autumn of 1903, the Honourable Artillery Company made an historic fraternal visit to Boston, the "Cradle of Liberty". No British soldier had set foot in the American city since Independence had been declared in 1776, so the significance of this visit was not lost on someone as mindful of the past as Erskine Childers. But that significance was rapidly eclipsed by his falling in love, virtually at first sight, with Mary Alden Osgood, known to all as Molly, the lively daughter of a family distinguished in Boston life since settling there from England in 1648.

Their wedding in 1904 was a highlight of the Boston social calendar, and they returned to London knowing that Molly's father, the distinguished surgeon Hamilton Osgood, wished to buy them a new cruising boat as a wedding present provided that she found she shared her new husband's passion for sailing. This was quite a challenge, for Childers was fearful that a disability in walking, which was the legacy of a childhood injury, would make sailing impossible for his bride. But a trial cruise in the 15-ton yawl *Sunbeam,* in which he owned a third share, revealed that Molly was a natural sailor with a particular talent for helming, and so the order for the new boat was placed with Colin Archer.

Designer and client put everything they knew into this very special yacht. Archer was nothing if not versatile, as had been shown by his racing yachts and the design of Nansen's *Fram*. So although the basic inspiration for the hull shape showed the influence of Archer's ablest sailing lifeboats, very quickly the new vessel acquired her own unique character. As with any new one-off boat, the design was modified as construction proceeded, and although Archer's "final" *Asgard* design, dated February 1905, is now in the archives of the *Norsk Sjofartsmuseum* in Oslo, even at that late stage Childers was requesting modifications, including the insertion – not shown in the plans in the Oslo archive – of a bridge-deck between the small aft cabin top and the main cabin top over the saloon.

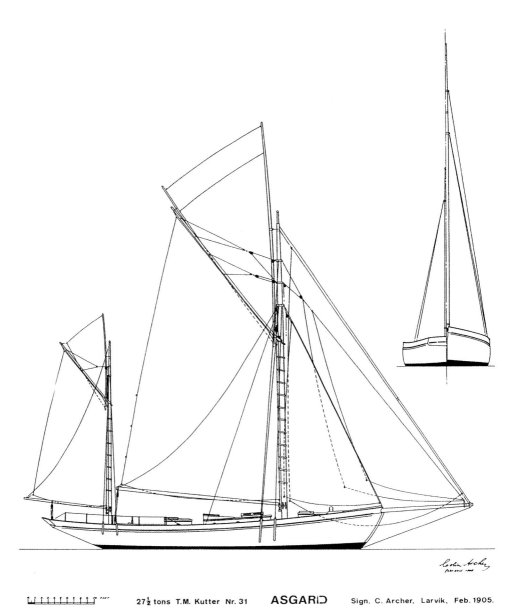

27½ tons T.M. Kutter Nr. 31   **ASGARD**   Sign. C. Archer, Larvik, Feb. 1905.

While *Asgard* may have borne a superficial resemblance to Colin Archer's rescue boats and exploration vessels, she was in fact a remarkably sophisticated design with an excellent turn of speed allied to exceptional sea kindliness.

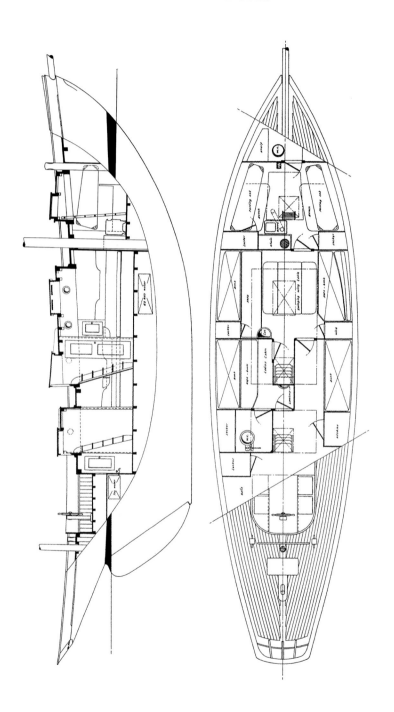

Asgard LOA 51ft, LWL 38ft, Beam 13ft. Draft 6.75ft, TM 28 tons.

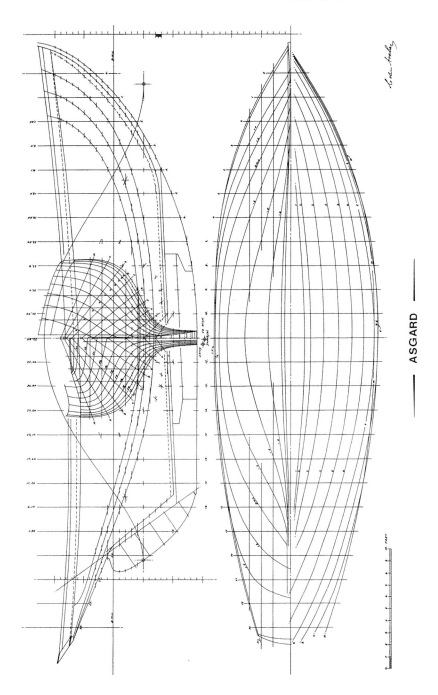

ASGARD

Asgard gliding along in near-calm conditions during a cruise to the Baltic by Erskine and Molly Childers in 1906. This photo well illustrates how lightly she floated in her original form, before she had become laden with an auxiliary engine and then later with the extra accommodation and equipment needed for her subsequent role as a sail training vessel.

Asgard was so named in honour of her Scandinavian origins – "Asgardr" is the Norse word for Home of the Gods, the land between heaven and earth. As well, a modest pun was implied on Osgood, the name of the donor. But however named, she was indeed a Ship of the Gods, and proved notably comfortable at sea, though to modern eyes the old-fashioned location of the galley well forward would seem to invite unnecessary discomfort while cooking in a seaway. Nevertheless both Erskine and Molly were renowned for the quality of the food they were both personally able to create in this cramped little foc's'le. And they had ample opportunity to do this. Although his parliamentary duties meant that Childers had to retain a professional delivery skipper to bring the new boat from Norway to the south of England in the summer of 1905, on the last day of August the young couple had their first sail on their new dreamship, and in the years which followed they cruised as often as a growing family and other interests would permit, with the Baltic a favourite destination.

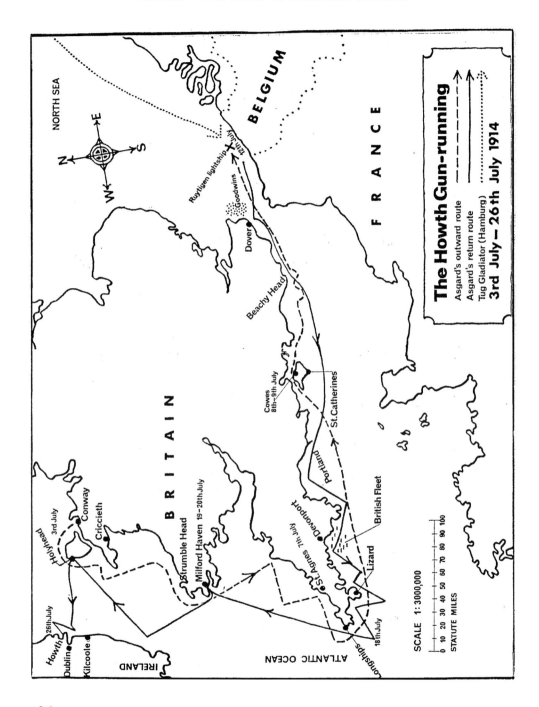

The Howth Gun-running

Asgard's outward route
Asgard's return route
Tug Gladiator (Hamburg)

3rd July – 26th July 1914

Those "other interests" included Childers' growing support for Home Rule for Ireland, an enthusiasm encouraged by Molly whose growing affection for the country was fuelled by regular visits to the Bartons in Glendalough House. In 1911 the publication of his book, *The Framework of Home Rule,* placed Childers' viewpoint on the record. There was much goodwill among their friends in London towards the concept, and life continued on its agreeable course, with their most ambitious cruise aboard *Asgard* being undertaken in 1912-13. This took them through the Baltic to Finland, and then back to Norway. *Asgard* was left in Oslo for their friend Gordon Shephard to make a return cruise. That cruise in the Autumn of 1913 became something of a struggle, for Shephard in typical style wished to make it as interesting as possible, so he came home by way of the Outer Hebrides. October became November, and the weather was ferocious. Eventually, a somewhat bedraggled *Asgard* finished her season in Bangor in North Wales, and in due course Gordon Shephard was declared the 1913 winner of the world's most senior annual cruising trophy, the Challenge Cup of the Royal Cruising Club, for this rugged bit of sailing achievement.

Meanwhile, the going was becoming tough in the movement towards Home Rule. November 1913 saw the formation of the Irish Volunteers under Eoin MacNeill in support of the modest level of Home Rule which had been proposed for the third time by the House of Commons in London, but was being thwarted by the House of Lords, and actively opposed by the Ulster Volunteers. With a worsening situation, on December 4th 1913 the Government in London prohibited the importation of arms and ammunition into any part of Ireland. But in defiance of this, on 24th April 1914 the Ulster Volunteers landed some 20,000 German rifles and three million rounds of ammunition at Larne in County Antrim.

Until then, the Irish Volunteers had been totally law-abiding in their support for Home Rule. But in view of the Larne gun-running, it was becoming increasingly obvious that some significant gesture in Ireland in support of parliamentary democracy in London was necessary to stiffen

Gordon Shephard and Erskine Childers aboard *Asgard*
sailing down the English Channel with their
consignment of vintage rifles, July 1914.

morale. Government patrols to prevent gun-running had been stepped up after the northern episodes, which made the use of ships or fishing boats impossible if any arms shipment was envisaged, however modest in scope. Thus yachts offered the only way.

Down in the Shannon Estuary, Conor O'Brien at Foynes began preparing his old ketch *Kelpie,* while Childers volunteered the *Asgard.* Her rigging needed a major overhaul after Gordon Shephard's adventures the previous Autumn, but after some difficulties both vessels arrived on schedule on July 12th 1914 at the Ruytigen Lightship off the Belgian coast to collect 1500 ancient rifles from a waiting tugboat.

The *Asgard* had a very able crew of Erskine and Molly Childers, Gordon Shephard, Conor O'Brien's cousin Mary Spring Rice from Foynes, and two experienced Donegal seamen, Charles Duggan and Pat McGinley from Gola Island. Thus although the long voyage back to Ireland was diabolically uncomfortable with their little ship crowded out with 900 rifles, the *Asgard* was able to make the splendidly dramatic and effective gesture of sweeping under sail into the harbour of Howth northeast of Dublin in broad daylight on Sunday July 26th 1914, and the 900 guns were unloaded with the help of the Volunteers in just 45 minutes.

A more complex plan evolved for O'Brien's cargo. Another leading Home Rule enthusiast with an interest in sailing was the Limerick-born Sir Thomas Myles, an eminent Dublin surgeon. Unlike *Asgard* and *Kelpie,* his yacht the *Chotah* had an auxiliary engine, which provided the capacity for prolonged manoeuvring off an open beach. So the *Kelpie's* guns were transferred to the *Chotah* at a hidden anchorage off the Welsh coast, and the entire cargo was then successfully discharged onto the isolated beach at Kilcoole on the Wicklow coast on the night of Saturday 1st August 1914.

However, within a week, global events took over. The Great War broke out, and all the leading partici-pants in the gun running joined the British forces, partly in the belief that they were fighting for the rights of small nations. Childers became a highly decorated Lt. Commander in the Royal Navy, and then went on to a notable naval flying career. Shephard in 1917 became the youngest Brigadier in the British Army, but died on active service with the Royal Flying Corps in January 1918. Myles joined the Royal Army Medical Corps, and swiftly rose to the rank

Molly Childers and Mary Spring Rice determinedly displaying the cargo aboard *Asgard,* July 1914.

of Colonel. And O'Brien soon found his niche with mine-sweepers in the Royal Naval Volunteer Reserve, and served with distinction for the duration.

By the time that duration was completed in November 1918, Ireland was in turmoil. The War of Independence led to a Treaty in December 1921, which in turn led to Civil War. Erskine Childers, who had returned to Ireland in 1917 to become involved at the highest levels of leadership and negotiation, had by this time progressed from favouring a modest level of Home Rule to outright support for total independence, and ended up fighting for the anti-Treaty Forces.

In the thick of it..........an exhausted Erskine Childers (right) and Mary Spring Rice (back to camera) during the unloading of the guns at Howth

With their defeat in 1922, he went on the run. The beleaguered new Free State Government passed a law making the carrying of any guns punishable by execution. Childers was captured in Glendalough House in Annamoe carrying a miniature hand gun, originally a present from his former friend Michael Collins, who had been killed while leading the pro-Treaty forces. On the

Erskine Childers towards the end of his life.

morning of November 24th 1922 in Dublin, an hour later than planned in order to comply with the prisoner's request that he be allowed to see the sunrise, Robert Erskine Childers was executed by firing squad. Before being blindfolded, he had shaken hands with each one of them in turn. His last words were: "Take a step or two forward, lads. It will be easier that way."

In a country now weary of war, life slowly took on a new semblance of normality. In time, after living for many years at their family home at Terenure in south Dublin, Erskine Childers' widow Molly was to settle at Glendalough House in Annamoe, where she lived until her death in 1964. Conor O'Brien, who was less extreme in his views than Childers, and had been prepared to work for the new Free State Government as a Fisheries Inspector using his old *Kelpie* to range along the west coast, took off on his great voyage round the world with his new *Saoirse* in 1923. But although he saw this partly as a maritime celebration of Ireland's newly independent status, maritime realities in the fledgling state were not encouraging. There was little sign of any real

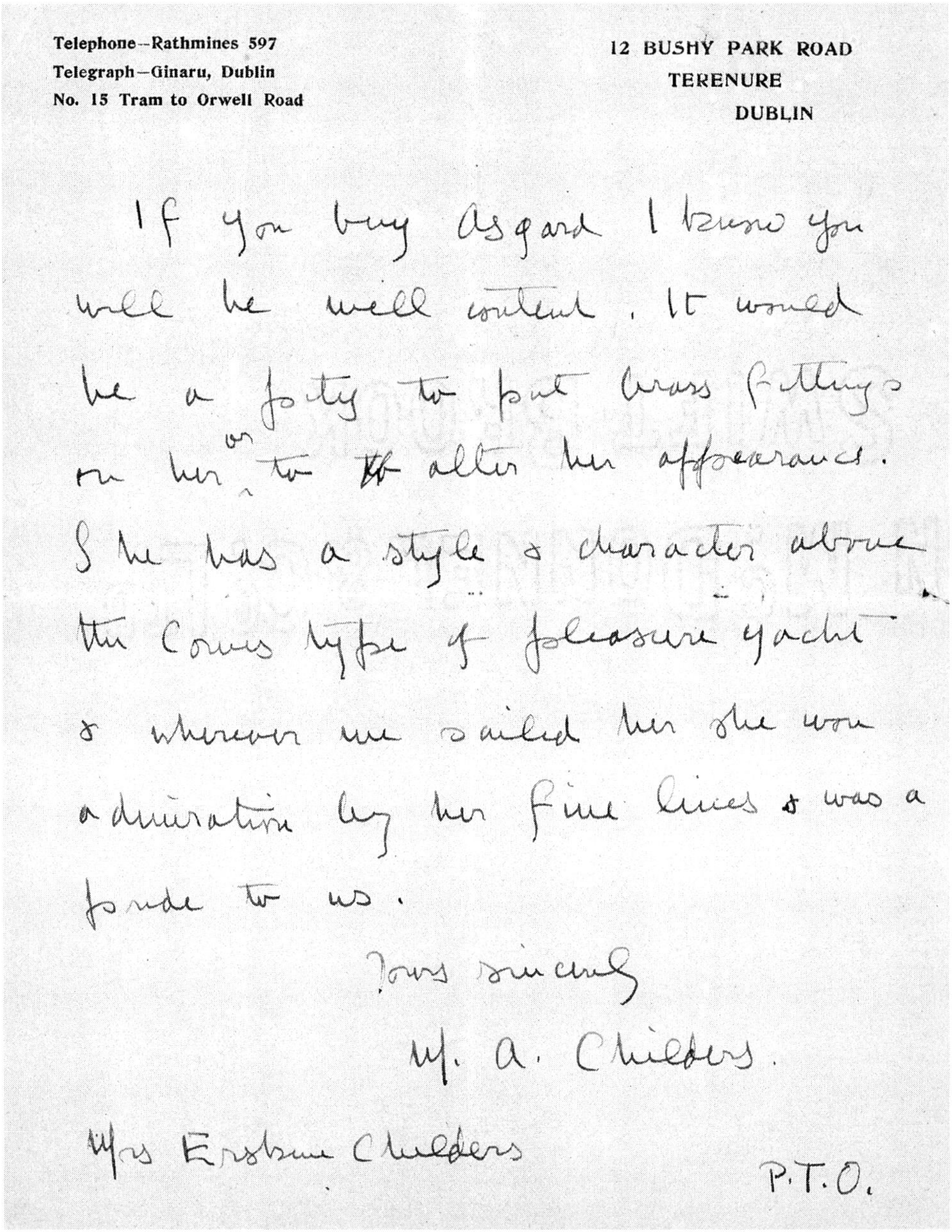

Telephone—Rathmines 597
Telegraph—Ginaru, Dublin
No. 15 Tram to Orwell Road

12 BUSHY PARK ROAD
TERENURE
DUBLIN

If you buy Asgard I know you will be well content. It would be a pity to put brass fittings on her or to alter her appearance. She has a style & character above the Cowes type of pleasure yacht & wherever we sailed her she won admiration by her fine lines & was a pride to us.

Yours sincerely

M. A. Childers.

Mrs Erskine Childers

P.T.O.

Page from a letter written on 15th May 1928 by Molly Childers to Mr & Mrs John Mulock of Cornwall, when they were contemplating the purchase of *Asgard*.

fulfilment of national seafaring potential, and *Asgard's* role in the creation of the new state seemed largely forgotten.

Asgard had been laid up in North Wales in 1914 immediately after the Howth gun running. It was not until 1927 that Molly Childers could bring herself to put the beloved ketch on the market, and in the early summer of 1928 she was sold by Dickie's Boatyard of Bangor in North Wales to an English owner, John Mulock of Truro in Cornwall. In a friendly exchange of letters, Mrs Childers hoped that he would retain the name, and John Mulock complied with this request. Writing on May 15th 1928 from Terenure, Molly Childers

Freed of her cargo, *Asgard* quickly gathers speed as she turns to windward through the mouth of Howth Harbour on the afternoon of Sunday July 26th 1914. The ketch is sailing well despite being reduced to a gaff-topped trisail after her mainsail had been damaged in the unloading of the guns. She was not seen again in Howth for 47 years.

Asgard in 1937, when the Mulock family bought her for the second time, and gave her an extensive refit with glossy black topsides.

remained enthusiastic about the ship: "*Asgard* has splendid sea-going qualities —
sturdy, quick in stays, & sensitive to her helm. We have cruised with her in
many waters, & she never failed us … she has a style & character above the
Cowes type of pleasure yacht, & wherever we sailed her she won admiration
for her fine lines & was a pride to us."

Under the ownership of John Mulock and his wife from 1928 to 1932,
Asgard became a familiar sight in the waters of the English West Country,
usually based at Fowey on the south coast of Cornwall, but re-fitted each
winter at the noted shipyard port of Appledore on the north Devon coast. With
tanned sails and her hull painted gleaming black in some seasons, she acquired
something of a new identity. But even so, she was still widely recognised as
Erskine Childers' yacht, and in those waters, he was more widely remembered

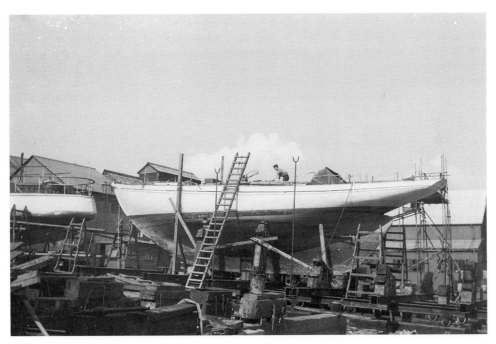

The lines of a thoroughbred. *Asgard* re-fitting in 1960 for a proposed Transatlantic cruise
which fortunately never happened

Homeward bound. *Asgard* departs in calm conditions under power from Southampton on 21st July 1961, bound for Howth with Tom Cronin on the helm. It was the first time she had flown the tricolour of the Republic.

as the author of *The Riddle of the Sands,* rather than as someone who had met a tragic end in the Irish Civil War.

In 1932, *Asgard* passed into the ownership of a friend of the Mulock family, Major W.B.Branston. However, although he lavished care on the ship and installed an auxiliary engine, he kept her for only five years – in 1937 she was bought by John Mulock's brother, Lt Col C.E. Mulock, and in 1947 he installed a new auxiliary engine, and electric light as well. He continued to cruise her in the waters sailed by his brother, mainly in the western part of the English Channel and across to Brittany. But in 1958, when the constraints of advancing age made him decide to give up offshore sailing, he put *Asgard* on the market.

She was bought by a Canadian called Hughes, who planned to sail her to the Caribbean. With the needs of this venture in mind, the new owner planned a major refit for *Asgard* in a boatyard near the Mulocks' home at Truro on the upper reaches of the Fal Estuary. Unfortunately, this ambitious project soon began to run into financial problems, and Colonel Mulock was concerned to note that his family's beloved old boat, now enduring her third lengthy lay-up, was by 1960 beginning to show signs of serious neglect. But help was at hand – eventually – from Ireland.

It had taken a long time for "official Ireland" to start to look to the sea. As outlined in Chapter 1, the Emergency of World War II in 1939 saw the creation of Irish Shipping and the beginnings of seamanship training schemes. When that war ended, the Maritime Inscription became the Naval Service in 1946, and the *Slua Muiri* – the "Sea Group" – was created as its voluntary reserve arm.

Naturally there was talk, as noted in Chapter 1, of the possibilities of sea training in general, and sail training in particular. And at the recreational level, the end of 1945 had seen the formation of the Irish Dinghy Racing Association, which in time became the Irish Yachting Association, and is today the Irish Sailing Association. From its earliest days, it set up Junior Training Programmes operating through the clubs throughout the country.

But although Jack Tyrrell may have produced his proposed design for a sail training barquentine in 1954, and though the first seeds of the international sail training movement may have been sown in 1956 with the Torbay to Lisbon Race, in Ireland it was enough, during the 1950s, merely to maintain a basic level of economic survival. The idea of a sail training ship seemed an absurd luxury. Yet there were those who became profoundly concerned with the fate of *Asgard,* and their interest led in time to a proper Irish sail training programme based on offshore sailing. But it was not until 21st March 1969 that *Asgard* was finally commissioned in Howth by Erskine Hamilton Childers, the son of her original owner, as Ireland's first official sail training vessel.

Asgard off the north coast of Lambay, July 24th 1961. She had so effectively demonstrated her speed on the passage from the Solent that she had to remain in hiding behind the island for two days before re-enacting the 1914 visit to Howth.

48

Yet it was in 1960 that the Irish journalist Liam MacGabhann had discovered her on the banks of the Truro River in Cornwall. Through his writings and with the support of some friends in places of influence, he persuaded the Irish government to purchase her. She was taken to Camper & Nicholson's famous yard in Southampton for a refit in preparation for the season of 1961, when she undertook the symbolic voyage back to Howth. Lt Joe Deasy, now Commodore Deasy and a retired Flag Officer Commanding the Naval Service, was skipper, helped by noted Howth sailor Tom Cronin – who had a commission in the *Slua Muiri* – and a combined Naval Service/ *Slua Muiri* crew. As others had found before, and were to find again, the *Asgard*

Taoiseach Sean Lemass salutes the colours at Howth on the day of *Asgard's* return.

surprised with her speed. The passage was much quicker than expected, and they had to spend some days hidden in the island anchorage of Swallow Cove at Lambay in order to arrive at the appointed time in Howth.

So it was that, on 26th July 1961 – 47 years to the day since the gun-running – *Asgard* sailed into Howth Harbour escorted by Naval Service vessels and Air Corps planes, to be greeted by a salvo of guns and a welcome from President Eamon de Valera. With his black silk top hat and austere demeanour, he was already redolent of a bygone era in an Ireland which was now rapidly changing. It was an Ireland, too, in which many were surprised to find that Molly Childers was still alive. But she was to continue to live at Glendalough

After 47 years, *Asgard* returns to Howth.

House in Annamoe until her death in 1964. So it was a vivid reminder of times past when Eamon de Valera sent her greetings from Howth in 1961 with the *Asgard* returned, his message concluding that "the great event in which she and her gallant husband took such a memorable part will never be forgotten by the Irish nation".

Asgard was used as a naval sail training vessel for a time during the early 1960s, but there was a significant amount of resistance in certain quarters in the Naval Service to her being so utilised, and increasingly the official line was that she was not regarded as very suitable for this purpose within the naval context. Nevertheless, enthusiastic sailing members of the *Slua Muiri* tried to

Surviving Volunteers in 1961 re-enact the 1914 landing of the guns.

get her organised for offshore racing and training cruises. But certain of the upper echelons of the Naval Service became ever more reluctant to permit such things. Once again – for the fourth time – the ketch was laid up ashore for a prolonged period, this time in the boatyard at the Coal Harbour in Dun Laoghaire.

However, she was soon in the news again, with various yachtsmen and journalists writing about the fate of this famous vessel, for the official line indicated that she might be preserved as no more than an immobile monument. Passions were aroused. Des Turvey, whose employment with *The*

President de Valera in the midst of the re-enactment at Howth, July 1961.

Irish Times was actually as an accountant, but who also wrote on sailing matters, leapt into print at every opportunity on the need to make proper use of *Asgard*, and treat her with the respect she deserved. And Sean Flood, recently Commodore of Clontarf Yacht & Boat Club and a former lieutenant in the *Slua Muiri*, who had much enjoyed sailing *Asgard* in her naval days with the legendary 17-footer helmsman "Buddy" Thompson, was another eloquent advocate of a policy of proper respect for the old ketch.

So gradually the tide was turned. An element of *Realpolitik* was brought to the problem when it was realised that the best hope of positive action was to be

Snapshot of a people entering a period of change. As President de Valera is escorted back to the state Rolls Royce after formally welcoming *Asgard* on her return to Howth in July 1961, his departure is witnessed by a crowd embodying Ireland's past, present and future.

53

found in targetting a leading figure in Government who was personally interested in the sea. Charles J. Haughey, himself a sailing enthusiast, was Minister for Finance at the time. With his support, the *Asgard* was taken under the wing of the Department of Finance. The Minister established *Coiste an Asgard* in 1968 and thus – at last – funds were made available to commission Erskine and Molly Childers' historic ketch as Ireland's first sail training vessel.

There was widespread concern at the lack of a clearcut policy for the use of *Asgard* after she had returned in 1961, and one of those who urged her use as a sail training ship was *Slua Muiri* S/Lt Sean Flood, seen here on the bridge of the corvette LE *Cliona* in the early 1960s.

3

The *Asgard* revolution

The ketch *Asgard* becomes Ireland's first sail training ship 1969

The modern secretariat of *Coiste an Asgard* is a busy and respected administrative unit, dealing confidently and competently with a throughput of trainees which runs into the hundreds and increasingly towards the thousand mark annually, while at the same time overseeing the myriad tasks involved in running a ship which sails many seas and regularly effects crew changes in distant ports.

As for the brigantine *Asgard II,* she is a much-loved flagship for the entire Irish maritime movement. Her visits to ports in Ireland are times of special civic pride allied in a uniquely Irish way with unstuffy conviviality, while her participation in the International Sail Training Association programme and other voyages abroad finds her functioning as a very successful roving ambassador spreading goodwill wherever she goes. Yet throughout this busy annual programme, she continues quietly to get on with the rewarding business of introducing young people from all parts of Ireland and from every walk of life to the wonders of sailing the sea on a traditionally-rigged ship.

Even at their most optimistic, the early members of *Coiste an Asgard* could scarcely have hoped that their pioneering efforts would be bearing such abundant fruit in such a relatively short time. For the splendid new brigantine *Asgard II* was to be commissioned in Arklow in March 1981. Yet it was only in March 1968, just thirteen years earlier, that the inaugural meetings of this new committee were being held to look at ways and means of implementing C. J. Haughey's recommendation to the Government – on February 2nd 1968 – that Erskine and Molly Childers' ketch *Asgard* become Ireland's first sail training vessel.

It says much for the Committee's trail-blazing efforts that, in such a short time, they were to change the Irish public attitude to sail training from one of ignorance and indifference into an enthusiastic acceptance and support of the concept of a national sail training ship. In fact, the change in public attitude was brought about in much less time than the thirteen years which elapsed between the first meeting of the Committee, and the commissioning of the purpose-built brigantine. For it was after only five years, in 1973, that government policy had already moved on to favour the building of a proper ship. The complexity of her concept and the financial restraints of public spending cuts may have meant that it was another eight years before the vessel was actually completed. But this in no way diminishes the scale of the remarkable change in public attitudes which the early work of *Coiste an Asgard* achieved. It was nothing less than an *Asgard* Revolution.

In the earliest days, the Committee's task was fraught with difficulty. Bluntly, the only opportunity to provide Ireland with a sail training scheme lay in determinedly utilising the *Asgard* and all the favourable public sentiment which she aroused. Yet in her original form as a classic cruising yacht of 1905, her accommodation and general layout below were unsuitable and inadequate, for in truth she was too small for the task envisaged.

But that same *Realpolitik* which had seen C.J.Haughey becoming *Asgard's* political patron was now deployed in turning her into as good a sail training ship as she could be within the limits of her size. It was no ordinary project, but *Coiste an Asgard* was no ordinary committee. In its way, it was remarkably representative of the early signs of the changes which were to lead over the next thirty years to Ireland becoming a vibrant modern state, for the original committee of five was largely made up of busy people in a hurry, people with a "can-do" approach to life.

Coiste an Asgard was particularly fortunate in its founding chairman, Frank Lemass, who was able in effect to run the *Asgard's* shoreside administration through his office as Chairman of CIE (*Coras Iompair Eireann,* the national transport authority) with the inspired assistance of his formidable secretary, Miss Keogh. As another first member of the Committee, Liam McGonagle, put it: "Basically, *Coiste an Asgard* in its early days was just Frank Lemass with a vision and an official chequebook, used sparingly but effectively. It was Frank Lemass who used all his charm, foresight and sense of purpose to get the ship quickly into commission. He provided the leadership and administrative skill which created and guaranteed the future of Irish sail training".

Frank Lemass 1912-1974) was of course the younger brother of Sean Lemass, whose elevation to Taoiseach in 1959 had begun the long process of Ireland's re-awakening. But the younger brother was very much his own man, and a formidable figure in the world of business and the administration of public utilities. Sailing was a passion with

Frank Lemass (1912 - 1974) founding Chairman of *Coiste an Asgard*. He is seen here at the helm of his Dragon class sloop *Aletta,* which was Ireland's Olympic Dragon in 1960.

Liam McGonagle (1929-1999), seen here at the helm of his 46ft ketch *Ounavarra* during his last cruise in August 1999, was another founder member of *Coiste an Asgard*

him, and he brought his superb management skills to it, being a Commodore of the National Yacht Club, a leading figure in the fledgling Irish Yachting Association as it emerged from the Irish Dinghy Racing Association, and an early organiser of Boat Shows, while also giving of his time for the Lifeboat Institution. Thus as far as Ireland's sailing community was concerned, it was Sean Lemass who was the brother of Frank Lemass.

His small committee was carefully chosen. Liam McGonagle, an experienced boat-owner and seafaring enthusiast who was subsequently to become one of the most successful Commodores of the Irish Cruising Club, was very much at the heart of things in Dublin's commercial, political and legal life. Like Frank Lemass, he was renowned for his ability to carry projects through to a successful conclusion, and in the 1980s he was to head the special committee which created the modern Howth Yacht

Club marina and club-house complex.

Cork's great maritime traditions were represented on the Committee by Clayton Love Jnr., one of the southern city's famed 'Merchant Princes'. A keen dinghy racer in the 1950s and 60s, he had already been the instigator of the changes which set the Irish Dinghy Racing Association along the road to becoming the Irish Yachting Association and subsequently the Irish Sailing Association, which is today a national sporting authority of exemplary effectiveness. At the time of the

Clayton Love Jnr has given unique service to *Coiste an Asgard,* as he was a founder member, and continues as a member thirty-two years later.

foundation of *Coiste an Asgard,* much of his energies were taken up in the business of merging the world's oldest yacht club, the Royal Cork at Cobh, with the more energetic Royal Munster YC at Crosshaven, in order to have one vibrant club in place for the Quarter Millennial Celebrations of the Royal Cork in 1970, for the club was the modern manifestation of the Water Club of the Harbour of Cork, founded in 1720.

Those hugely successful Quarter Millennial celebrations of the Royal Cork Yacht Club at Crosshaven were actually developed into a two-year affair in 1969 and 1970, including a Cruise-in-Company, several major championships and offshore races, and an early version of Cork Week. So inevitably the time that Clayton Love could give to *Coiste an Asgard* in its early days was rationed. But his advice was highly valued and today, more than thirty years later, he is the only one of the original membership still serving on the Committee. It is all part of a remarkable record of service to Ireland's maritime needs, for in 1969 he also joined the Committee of Management of the Royal National Lifeboat Institute, of which he was a member until 1999, when he retired having served additionally as Vice President since 1980, and Deputy Chairman since 1991.

The provision of a national sail training programme using a seagoing ship was a venture into uncharted waters, but already there was experience in

Brian Campbell (inset) played a key role in the inauguration and development of the Irish Yachting Association's Junior Training Programme in the early 1960s, based on his pioneering work with junior sailing in the Heron Class at several clubs on the north side of Dublin Bay, particularly as seen here at Kilbarrack, where the Heron prepare for racing in 1960 as the tide fills their sailing area inside Bull Island. Brian Campbell was appointed a founder member of *Coiste an Asgard* in March 1968. Since his retirement from a career in banking, he has given of his time working with overseas missions, notably with Mother Theresa in Calcutta.

training youngsters for racing purposes in inshore waters within the club-based structure of Irish sailing, using the Junior Programme devised by the Irish Yachting Association. One of the leading organisers and developers of that scheme was Brian Campbell from Sutton on the northern shores of Dublin Bay, and he too was signed on to *Coiste an Asgard*.

Finally, all that was best in Irish sailing in its broadest sense was represented by Dr Rory O'Hanlon, one of Dun Laoghaire's leading sailors. A distinguished member of the Royal St George YC, which he served as Commodore from 1966 to 1970, he was also a longterm member of the Irish Cruising Club, where he became Commodore from 1972 to 1975. As well, he was one of the few Irish members of the Royal Cruising Club, with which Erskine Childers had been much involved. Thus "The Rory" provided *Coiste an Asgard* with special

Rory O'Hanlon (1916 to 1980) was another noted figure who played a key role in the early years of *Coiste an Asgard*. Here, he is at the helm of his 43ft sloop *Clarion*, which he cruised to the Arctic and also sailed with cup-winning success in the Fastnet Race.

links to the most senior sailing establishments in both Ireland and Britain. This greatly strengthened the credibility of the old *Asgard's* new purpose in life. But even more importantly, it was Rory O'Hanlon who suggested that Eric Healy would be the ideal skipper for *Asgard* in her sail training role.

For it was abundantly clear that, in its early days at least, *Coiste an Asgard* would be functioning on limited funds. Not to put too fine a point on it, if the project was to succeed, the fulltime skipper would have to be someone of dedicated enthusiasm and personal resourcefulness accustomed to making do on very little in the way of resources, and operating largely on his own. Eric Healy was the man for the job.

Captain George Frederick Healy had been born in Dublin on February 7th 1927. As his father disliked both of his forenames, "Eric" was extracted from his second name, and he has been Eric ever since. His interest in the sea came partially from his mother's occasional involvement in sailing, but especially from the family's respect for the memory of his Great Uncle, also G.F. Healy, a Captain in the Orient Line who retired to become a Missionary, and had died in that calling at St Lucia in the Caribbean in 1933.

Like his Great Uncle, young Eric was to become a committed Anglican churchman. But as a young teenager in Ireland in the early war years, he felt frustrated in his hopes of pursuing a longterm career in the international merchant marine. A friend of his father suggested enrolment in England in the Thames Nautical Training College, which in peacetime had utilised the ship HMS *Worcester*. It was an attractive proposition. At that time, a Merchant Navy Cadet/Apprentice had to complete four years at sea before sitting his Second Mate's Certificate. But one year of this four year term could be waived for every two years of attendance at a recognised training establishment, while the demands for manpower in the war years, and in the immediate post-war years as well, meant that a further year could be waived with the issue of a temporary Second Mate's Certificate on an annual basis.

So at the age of 16 in 1943, Eric Healy found himself moving from a state of youthful frustration in Dublin into the fast lane of education and promotion in the merchant marine with a two year course in the Thames Nautical Training College. Although a mercantile marine establishment, Thames Nautical College was run on fairly strict Naval lines and discipline. Its headquarters were in a large house at Sidcup in Kent, where a busy teaching routine saw the young Healy receiving a particularly sound training in navigation. But as well, the boys had frequent sailing in dinghies in a flooded quarry nearby, while great emphasis was put on practical time on ships. The famous tea clipper *Cutty Sark* was also laid up nearby, with her basic rig still in place, and she too was pressed into service by the Thames Nautical College for seamanship training, so much so that in later years the skipper of the *Asgard* occasionally let drop the information that he had served on the *Cutty Sark* …

World War II was still in its final messy weeks when Eric Healy graduated from the Thames Nautical Training College at the age of 18, and signed on as a Cadet on his first ship, T.S.S. *Lanarkshire,* which was bound from Scotland to Australia in what was to be one of the last convoys of the war. His first job was as operator of the special VHF Radio (very much a novelty in those days) which had been installed on each ship in the convoy to aid the maintenance of positions. Thus within three years of leaving Ireland, he had become competent in advanced navigation and the latest in radio technology, and he spent two happy and instructive Cadet years with the *Lanarkshire's* owners, the Clan Line, which had regular cargo liner routes from Britain

"Back to school…." – the youthful Eric Healy works up his navigation at the Irish Nautical Training College.

to South and East Africa, Australia and India with ships which were a byword for good on-board conditions.

Clan Buchanan at Port Said in the approaches to the Suez Canal, December 1947. Eric Healy served as Fourth Mate on *Clan Buchanan,* and was on board when this photo was taken.

As he had found it necessary to leave Ireland in order to get started in the merchant marine, it was appropriate that Eric Healy was one of the early peace-time benefi-ciaries of the Irish Nautical Training College which had been set up under Captain Tom Walsh in order to cope with the emergency manning requirements of Irish Shipping Ltd during the war. "The Emergency" may have been over, but Captain Walsh's College was still going strong in premises on Sir John Rogerson's Quay in the heart of Dublin, and in September 1947, Cadet Healy returned from service with the Clan Line to study for his Second Mates Certificate.

Tom Walsh was a fine teacher, and his little College was highly respected both at home and abroad. By December 1947, Eric Healy had been awarded his Temporary Second Mate's Certificate, which immediately enabled him to take up a new position as 4th Mate on the *Clan Buchanan.* A year later, he got his Full Certificate, and was promoted to Third Mate on the *Clan MacFarlane* at the age of 21. Then two years later, in the Autumn of 1950, he took his First Mate's certificate.

The frequency of his returns to Dublin meant that he became increasingly involved with the Dun Laoghaire sailing scene. The innovative sailor Douglas Heard, who was later to marry Eric's sister Ruth, was campaigning the advanced offshore racer *Huff of Arklow,* a 44ft sloop whose name reflected the fact that her design concept was three-quarters Uffa Fox, and one quarter Douglas Heard, while she was built by Jack Tyrrell in Arklow in 1950. Few if any of the amateur sailors in Dun Laoghaire had navigational qualifications to match those of Eric Healy, and he sailed on the *Huff* as navigator on offshore races which included several Royal Ocean Racing Club events both in the Irish Sea and the English Channel.

Rory O'Hanlon, who was a great friend and regular shipmate of Douglas Heard, thus became acquainted with Eric Healy and aware of the progress through life of the young Irish ship's officer. And it was a decidedly diverse progress before he returned to Ireland in 1968 on Rory's suggestion to become skipper-designate of *Asgard*. In 1953, he had yet again returned to Tom Walsh's

Douglas Heard's ultra-modern offshore racer *Huff of Arklow,* designed by Uffa Fox and built by Jack Tyrrell at Arklow in 1950.

Nautical College, by now located on the West Pier in Dun Laoghaire, this time to take his Master's Certificate. He qualified in October 1953, and availed of the opportunity to do an intensive Radar and VHF procedure course with the Royal Navy, which later proved invaluable.

Within two years the company had promoted him to First Mate, or Chief Officer as it is more usually known, at the age of 28. It was a particularly interesting time to be working for the Clan

Line, as they specialised in heavy lifts, and thus he was involved in such projects as shipping transformers for the new Kariba Dam, locomotives for the developing African railways, and complete fishing boats to Bangladesh. Further variety was provided by shipping oranges from South Africa to Europe.

But after seven years as Chief Officer, a feeling of frustration was becoming evident. The world of shipping was changing, and promotional opportunities were fewer. He would eventually be given a command, but it would be a case of stepping into dead men's shoes. His interest in religion and church work such as the Missions to Seamen had if anything increased. As a bachelor, he had no immediate ties to restrict his options. He felt called to undertake some job which would better utilise his professional skills more directly in the service of his fellow men.

A friendly clergyman mentioned the possibility of skippering the local church vessel which was being built in Australia to serve the islands of Melanesia in the Western Pacific. Melanesia consists of two island groups, the Solomon Islands and the New Hebrides, now called Vanuatu. In the early 1960s, airports were virtually nonexistent, while roads were poor, so most communication among and around the islands was done by sea. Thus although the new 87ft *Southern Cross* was officially the Mission Ship to carry the Bishop of Melanesia around his enormous and sprawling diocese of islands, when young Captain Healy took on this, his first command, in late 1962, he found that his ship's complement when on tour invariably included a Doctor or Nursing Sister, together with the School Inspector and often a District Commissioner as well.

In many areas, the available charts were of limited accuracy and not sufficient for local navigation, but in any case Diocesan funds did not run to having a complete and up-to-date set. So *Southern Cross's* skipper became adept at creating his own charts. As well, from time he time he found himself in command of what was in effect a hospital ship, or at least a floating ambulance. And then as term began or ended at the boarding school which was the only secondary school in the islands, he had the job of ferrying the pupils to and

Southern Cross, Eric Healy's first command – he is at the binnacle above the bridge. Built in 1961 as a Mission Ship for the Bishop of Melanesia, most appropriately for a vessel with an Irish skipper she was constructed in Ballina, albeit Ballina in New South Wales in Australia. *Southern Cross* was 87ft LOA, and powered by two 114bhp Gardner diesels.

from their often very distant home villages in remote islands. In all, it was wellnigh perfect training for skippering an Irish training vessel.

As 1968 approached, Eric Healy was due an extended leave after five years service. But in any case he reckoned the time had come for one of the islanders to take over command of the *Southern Cross*. He had sailed with a regular crew of 14, and several were now well able for the task. So before leaving for Ireland, Captain Healy told the Bishop that he hoped only to return to the islands in the distant future purely for holiday purposes, for the time was ripe for a Melanesian skipper to take charge. This came to pass. And so, back in

Ireland, Eric Healy was available and uniquely qualified to be appointed as the first skipper of *Asgard* in her new sail training role.

She underwent the necessary major modifications for this at remarkable speed. A traditional boatyard might have baulked at some of the things which had to be done, and would have found it difficult to keep to *Coiste an Asgard's* demanding schedule. But it so happened that at the otherwise sleepy estuary port of Malahide north of Dublin, the local boatyard had been taken over by the dynamic duo of Alf Tyaransen and Jack Fielding, a couple of contrasting characters who had arrived from Manchester in England. Alf – a Norwegian – was an ebullient fireball of energy and enthusiasm, while Jack was quiet and retiring. Between them, they had built up an extraordinary business. This had started with the conversion of retired trawlers into yachts, but they were now constructing purpose-built trawler-style yachts based on new hulls. Some of these were built in Norway, but most were built in Portugal to be towed across the Bay of Biscay for luxurious completion in Malahide.

The yard worked at prodigious speed, and in Myles Stapleton they had a talented in-house naval architect with the ability to transform their diverse customers' many requirements into handsome seagoing vessels. In some cases, they were obliged to install small operating theatres in order that the owners could avail of tax breaks allowed for charitable hospital ships … no problem, all

things were possible at Malahide Shipyard. So it was there, in the winter of 1968-69, that *Asgard* was converted for sail training needs.

Despite the modern speed with which it was achieved, it was never-theless organised in

Asgard among the big trawler yachts in Malahide Shipyard distinctly Irish style. The

Jack Gibney's pub in Malahide became for several years the meeting place of *Coiste an Asgard*. While the exterior, as seen in this photo from 1999, is largely unchanged, the interior has been considerably enlarged since the *Asgard* days.

pace of work was such that key members of the Committee had to inspect the boat at least once a week, so the pleasant routine developed of assembling on board *Asgard* each Saturday morning in the shed to monitor progress, and then adjourning to Jack Gibney's pub, a tiny place in those days, in the heart of Malahide village to review progress and discuss any queries which had arisen about the subsequent week's work programme.

Myles Stapleton would be on hand throughout these gatherings to explain the work and take notes, but as the members of *Coiste an Asgard* were a notably convivial crew, he admits that things tended to became somewhat hazy as they worked their way towards Any Other Business. But it proved such an effective way of getting the work done that the *Asgard* Committee continued to meet at Gibney's for several years afterwards. And in 1968-69, it all happened so quickly, with *Asgard*'s 1905 interior being literally gutted, that when some 27 years later we tried to draw plans of *Asgard*'s original interior working with Myles Stapleton, he confessed that he couldn't

69

remember much about the layout at all, it had all been cleared out in a matter of days, and he was working on several trawler yachts at the same time.

As a change from the "Malahide mayhem", one of Eric Healy's additional tasks was the careful assembly of all *Asgard's* gear, which had been stored with fastidious Naval Service care in various locations. Thus while *Asgard's* beautifully panelled interior, which had been witness to so much, was being chucked onto the scrapheap of history at breakneck pace in order to provide a usable sail training vessel on time, by contrast he found himself carefully signing

documents in triplicate at the Office of Public Works yard in Dun Laoghaire for Joe Gaynor, and at the *Slua Muiri* section in Cathal Brugha Barracks for Chief Petty Officer Michael Tracy, in order that the spars, rig and gear could be moved to the very different world of Malahide Boatyard.

Speed was of the essence, for the first trainee – Malcolm Fitzell of Dublin – had applied to join as early as March 6th 1968, when the *Asgard* project had been initially unveiled. In the fullness of time, he was to become one of *Asgard's* keenest watch leaders. Through the following winter, a series of talks at schools and sailing clubs had expanded the list of potential trainees, and created the nucleus of a corps of watch officers and leaders who were prepared to devote

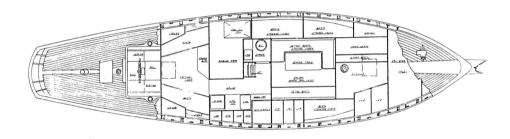

Asgard as she was re-developed by Myles Stapleton of Malahide Shipyard to serve as a sail training vessel

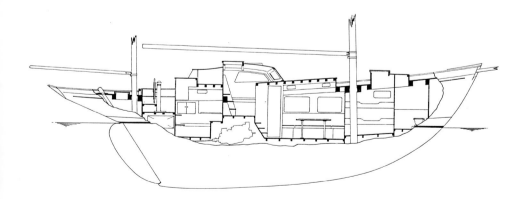

71

Asgard's first trainee was Malcolm Fitzell. He is now a geologist, but continues to sail.

their time to making the new scheme work.

With the interior empty, the new layout – with extra bunks, and the galley moved to a much more easily worked location amidships – could be quickly installed by the Malahide shipwrights. As well, a new Parsons Pike diesel auxiliary was fitted. Though it gave useful drive, the fact that the propeller had to be fitted under the port quarter, rather than on the centre-line, sometimes resulted in eccentric handling characteristics under power at slow speeds.

Space was decidedly limited for a sail training vessel, so Myles Stapleton deployed all his talents in creating a deckhouse which significantly improved the accommodation. It is impossible to see how it could have been done any better, and it was a very effective and comfortable feature which facilitated shelter and chart work, and also provided an invaluable extra bunk for shorter trainees.

Despite the changes, the *Asgard* as she emerged from Malahide in March 1969 was still recognisably the *Asgard* which had sailed into Howth in July 1914. She may have been fitted with a platform bowsprit in order to increase trainee safety, and the deckhouse, designed by Myles Stapleton in the style

While *Asgard's* layout and accommodation may have been significantly changed, on the slipway at Malahide she was still unmistakably the *Asgard* as built for Erskine and Molly Childers in 1905.

The new deckhouse greatly improved the comfort below

which he knew his shipwrights could most quickly build, may have had a whiff of modernity about it. But overall she was still a gaff rigged ketch, her peerless Colin Archer hull was totally unchanged in its sweeping lines, and the sense of the past moving into synergy with a new sail training future created a fresh mood of excitement.

It was a sense of excitement, however, which was not totally shared by the Howth fishermen. Being the weekend, their boats were as usual crowded into the small section of Howth's West Pier which at that time had the only area of deep water in the harbour. It had proved impossible to comply with requests to leave room available for *Asgard* to be commissioned in her new role alongside the West Pier. But this proved to be an advantage. For, instead of being semi-invisible in against the pier, *Asgard* was moored in mid-harbour to become a handsome floating platform.

From her masthead for the first time there fluttered the new *Asgard* burgee. This was a striking design by sailing artist and cartoonist Bob Fannin, inspired by pre-Celtic stone carvings together with variations on a Nordic *rune,*

The Commissioning of *Asgard* as a sail training vessel, Saturday 21st March 1969 –
C. J. Haughey is making a speech while Frank Lemass emerges from the companionway,
and Liam McGonagle is to starboard in the cockpit.

Thirty years on ... Eric Healy and Bob Fannin in October 1998 with the original
Asgard burgee, which was designed with inspiration from pre-Celtic carvings
by Bob Fannin in October 1968.

depicting a sun and moon theme representing freedom in a timeless design
which seems as fresh today as it did on Saturday 21st March 1969.

That day had its own special excitement, as the mid-harbour location, with
cables for the microphones for the public address systems being led through the
water to the *Asgard,* surely carried a certain risk of electrocution for anyone
speaking to the crowd on the pier. But fate smiled on this novel ceremony for
the Ship of the Gods. Speakers such as Frank Lemass and C.J. Haughey came
through unscathed. Then, nearly 55 years after *Asgard* had first sailed into
Howth on a very different mission, Erskine Hamilton Childers spoke to give
the official declaration that his father's and mother's yacht was now Ireland's
sail training vessel.

4 Moving mountains...

Asgard as a Sail Training Ship, 1969-1974

"We were making it up as we went along, and we were moving mountains". In that wry comment, one of the founder members of *Coiste an Asgard* sums up the experiences of the early years of Ireland's sail training programme with the original *Asgard*. For although the Sail Training Association programme was already developing internationally towards a level of activity which gave some indication of today's impressive and pervasive International Sail Training Association, in the Ireland of 1969 sail training was in its infancy, and everyone in the maritime world seemed to expect some sort of involvement at home with a little ship which was both a sail training vessel, and a very potent piece of Irish history.

Almost immediately, the limitations of the ketch's small size were becoming apparent. The original plan of introducing *Asgard* in her new role with a round Ireland cruise in the early part of the 1969 season had to be curtailed in Galway for several reasons, though the basic aim of giving West Coast crews experience and a sense of involvement with the vessel was well met. However, although she was easily able to make a round Ireland cruise, the original schedule was found to be overly ambitious. By the time local dignitaries and well wishers had been entertained aboard at the various ports visited, there was little enough time available for ongoing maintenance, for on a 51-footer even the most modest "civic reception" sometimes seemed to take over the entire vessel.

Early days of sailing in Dublin Bay, April 1969. The effortless way in which *Asgard* is slipping along (above) showed yet again just how skillfully Colin Archer had drawn her lines sixty-four years earlier. By 1969 Dublin Bay's last gaff-rigged class, the DBSC 21s, had already been converted to bermudan rig for six years, so sailing the *Asgard* was for many a novel experience (below), but soon Eric Healy and his crew were getting a good set for the tops'l (right).

With her new burgee proudly fluttering aloft, *Asgard* paces out past Holyhead Mountain in an inaugural event of the Irish Sea Offshore Racing Association.

As well, *Asgard* had not been in seagoing condition since 1964, so inevitably all of 1969's programme was something of a shakedown cruise, and an introduction to the realities of a very limited budget. In those earliest days, the stark reality was that the "*Asgard* Office" was no more than a filing cabinet in Frank Lemass's office, for the members of *Coiste an Asgard* shared their Chairman's view that their extremely scarce resources should be utilised almost entirely for direct expenditure on the ship and her equipment. Thus in the day-to-day sailing of the ketch, Eric Healy soon learnt that he and his crew were very much on their own. "We only heard from the 'Office' if there was something good about us in some newspaper" he recalls, "or if somebody had complained. Other than that, we seldom heard from them between crew changes at all. But it all added to the character-building aspect of the programme if the ship's company operated on a system of self-reliance, coupled with make do and mend when necessary."

In its way, this system was highly effective, for the early trainees developed a remarkable *esprit de corps* which, in some cases, was so enthusiastic that when winter and springtime maintenance and refitting was under way, Captain Healy knew that he could call on former shipmates for their help on a weekend of voluntary work. It became part of the "*Asgard* Ethos," and today you will meet mature sailing folk whose skill in maintaining their own craft can be traced directly back to those days of hard work on the old *Asgard*.

Despite the problems, *Asgard* logged many sailing miles in 1969, and in looking for seagoing objectives, she competed in a couple of offshore races in the Irish Sea, albeit with limited success against the new breed of offshore racer. More successful was an expedition to the south of England to take part in a Sail Training Association race from Portsmouth across the English Channel to Cherbourg. In those still relatively early days of the STA, numbers were small, but though the advent of *Asgard* brought the fleet numbers up to thirteen, she enjoyed good luck and placed second.

From that fortuitous beginning, there have blossomed very many years of happy international involvement as *Coiste an Asgard* has developed its

Shipboard routine as *Asgard* settles into her new career as a sail training vessel. Eric Healy (above) explains the intricacies of chartwork in the comfortable re-designed saloon. Traditional sounding methods (below left) using a leadline, while going aloft (below right) used an equally traditional bos'un's chair. Once she had started sailing at speed, the excitement of helming this fine vessel was an experience never forgotten (right)

operations, while the Sail Training Association itself has become the ISTA. But although such overseas ventures were important, in 1969 it was essential that experience and awareness of sail training be steadily developed in Ireland, where it was also important that the "yachting establishment" was courted. So another of *Asgard's* introductory duties was to serve as Committee Boat at both the Irish Yachting Association Dinghy Week in Baltimore, and a major international championship of the 505 dinghy class in Dun Laoghaire. As well, she was a participant in the Royal Cork YC Quarter Millennial Cruise-in-Company on Ireland's southwest coast, which drew in seagoing craft from both sides of the Atlantic.

All of this helped to increase the sailing public's awareness of *Asgard's* presence, but as Eric Healy recalls, it most emphatically wasn't what sail training should be all about. Committee Boat duties involved trainees in cleaning the ship each evening after the race officers had hosted their inevitable post-race party, which was scarcely an inspiring chore. As for the Cruise-in-Company, the other crews tended to be mature and experienced sailors intent on partying, rather than youthful trainees keen to learn about sailing. In neither case was it a healthy situation. Nevertheless it was all part of the necessary introductory process, for in the early years of the *Asgard* programme, *Coiste an Asgard* had to rely almost totally on Ireland's yacht clubs and the sailing community to provide able watch leaders and people with sufficient love of sailing to tolerate the old ketch's undoubted short-comings.

The 1969 season drew to its close with intensive watch leader training, and then during the winter another happy tradition was inaugurated with the first *Asgard* Reunion. Frank Lemass – with typical foresight and diplomacy – organised the use of the CIE Club in the heart of Dublin as a venue which was friendly, yet wasn't a club within the slightly daunting sailing establishment. Jerseys with the *Asgard* pennant were presented to the top trainees and watch leaders, Des Barrington showed his film of the launching, the commissioning ceremony, and life aboard, supper cost six shillings a head, and *Asgard* had come through her first sail training year.

While 1969 had not been without its problems, *Asgard* was now firmly established in her new role, and the Committee could plan for the 1970 season with some confidence. They decided that *Asgard* would be totally devoted to sail training. She was now well known to the sailing community, and in any case it was unbecoming for her to serve as a Committee Boat for an entire series. While this decision was reached as a sensible reaction to the experiences of 1969, it was the beginning of the process whereby, in due course, the new brigantine *Asgard II* was to become a flagship for the Irish maritime movement – slightly aloof perhaps, but a vessel of style which honours with any visit.

There was, however, a long way to go before *Asgard II* could fit so elegantly into such an important role, and much of that long way was covered by the first *Asgard* between 1970 and 1974. For 1970, the cost per day for trainees went up from £1 to 25 shillings, but they certainly were getting their money's worth. Making a round Ireland cruise in the early part of the season, Eric Healy recalls, "we went up just about every river estuary possible in the west of Ireland".

And they visited every port possible too, and built up a local chain of supporters right round the coast. The local pilots, great characters every one of them, also became enthusiastically involved. "It provided the scheme with good publicity" Eric Healy recalls, "it was great fun, and local people were able to see their vessel at work. I remember the great welcome we received at Cahirciveen. A local fisherman had piloted us up the Cahir River from Knightstown on Valencia Island. The whole town turned out at Cahirciveen to welcome us, including the local band. This was the way it was all along the western seaboard. The smaller the place, the greater the welcome."

"Further north, in Mayo, before going up the river to Westport at the head of Clew Bay, we anchored at Inish Lyre to pick up the local pilot, Tommy Gibbons. He and his family entertained us in their typical west of Ireland cottage. The anchorage at Inish Lyre is safe, but it is very isolated. To get to the nearest pub entailed a twenty minute boat journey, a ten minute walk along a track to the nearest road, and a half hour drive … In Westport itself, we were

Tad Minish was from Kentucky, but he loved the West of Ireland and lived there for many years. He was such an enthusiast for the *Asgard* ideal that he named his pub/restaurant at Westport Quay in honour of the ship. He is seen here sailing off the Connemara coast in his 36ft yawl *Kiff*, a Sparkman & Stephens design which was a sister ship of the famous *Finisterre*.

very well looked after by the late Tad Minish, an American from Kentucky who had settled in Mayo. He was so keen about the *Asgard* that he had got special permission to name his famous pub-restaurant in honour of the ship, and today the *Asgard* Bar & Restaurant on Westport Quay is one of the most popular establishments on the Connacht coast. Tad himself became much involved with our activities, and was appointed as one of our volunteer skippers."

"We went on around the Mayo coast to Sligo, where our pilot was the famous Austie Gillan, whose 200-year-old pub – Austie's at Rosses Point – continues to thrive. We got a great cheer for flying the code flag "H" to signal our requirement for a pilot, for as it happens, it is made up of the Sligo football club colours".

"One of our most interesting visits was to Burtonport, the little fishing port in The Rosses in northwest Donegal. We had anchored off Aranmore to await local advice on how to get into Burtonport, for in those days the entrance was even more intricate than it is now. A young local pilot offered to show us the way in, but when we arrived the pier was full of fishing vessels. Our pilot advised us where to anchor, and as it was high water I remarked that I thought it looked rather shallow, but he assured us it would be okay. Four hours later, we grounded, and started to heel over. The local TD was due on board for a visit, and we managed to entertain him despite the list. As the tide rose again, we came off unharmed, and berthed at the pier. I mentioned to one of the locals that the pilot had been mistaken about the depths, and he replied: "Don't blame him, he was told to anchor you there to draw the attention of the local TD to the fact that the harbour needs dredging". Sure enough, it was reported in the press that we had run aground. And since then, Burtonport has had at least two dredging schemes implemented, so maybe our brief experience of grounding did no harm at all."

"We changed crews at Burtonport, where we were joined by our first all-girl crew. Our next stop was Gola Island off Gweedore, home of the two Donegal sailors who had been aboard *Asgard* with Erskine Childers in 1914. The last of them, Pat McGinley, had recently died in New York, so all the local fishing boats took a day off fishing to accompany us as we sailed out to a wreath-laying ceremony in his honour, with the local parish priest dedicating the wreath. It was a moving occasion. Then the fishing boats returned to Burtonport, leaving *Asgard* on her own in the lovely anchorage at Gola. After the solemnity of the day's occasion, it seemed right and proper that we were now entertained by the last man living on Gola. He rowed out to us in a currach, and we welcomed him alongside. He presented us with goat's milk, and I offered him something stronger in return, which he was more than happy to accept. Aboard *Asgard,* he told us some great yarns of his experiences as a seaman all over the world, unconsciously changing his accent to match the location of each of his stories. It was a wonderfully entertaining evening, the

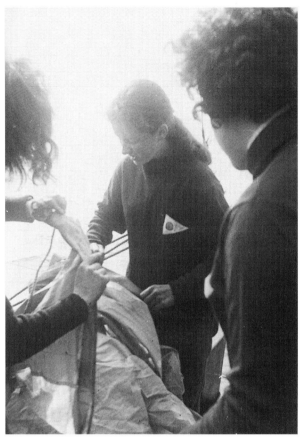

Asgard sailed with her first all-girl crew in 1970, and cruised with them from Donegal to Scotland and then on to Dun Laoghaire

perfect light-hearted conclusion to our west coast cruise. Next morning, we left Donegal, and sailed direct to Scotland, visiting Campbeltown and Stranraer before returning to Dun Laoghaire with our all-girl crew".

At the time, it was considered newsworthy that, for the first time in 1970, *Asgard* sailed with an all-girl crew, albeit with male watch leaders. It was thought necessary to gradually introduce the idea of female crews to Ireland's still very conservative general public even though, when owned by the Childers family, *Asgard* had often been very capably helmed by Molly Childers herself, while in the somewhat rarefied Irish sailing world of 1970, the presence of talented women sailors scarcely aroused comment, even if the yachting establishments in the older clubs still placed quaint restrictions on their membership.

For the latter part of the summer, it was away south and into the 1970 STA programme. A gale prevented *Asgard* making the start of the race from Weymouth to St Malo, but they still made the party at the finish in France.

Then at the end of July, new ground was broken with *Asgard's* first involvement in one of the longer STA races, from Plymouth across the Bay of Biscay to La Coruna. During this race, the first appearance of "Seamus", the *Asgard* mascot, was recorded — he was the creation of a medical student, who crafted him from sail-

Who did the washing up? Morning coffee for Eric Healy and an all-girl crew. A mizzen staysail has been set, although in light airs it tended to drape itself on top of the new deckhouse.

cloth. His shipmates meanwhile were learning of the ingenuity of the STA in making sense of their races, which have to cope with vessels of many different types. *Asgard* was still forty miles from the finish in La Coruna when the time limit expired, yet under the STA rules she not only was recorded as a finisher, but was placed fifth overall and won a cup for her troubles.

In fine form, the old ketch and her crew made a short celebratory cruise along the north Spanish coast, and found many of the STA fleet following them into a ria to join the Irish for a barbecue ashore. Then *Asgard* headed for home, and was caught up in her first real storm as a sail training ship while heading north towards Ireland in the vicinity of the Isles of Scilly. The mizzen mast was broken in atrocious conditions, but eventually shelter was found behind Lundy, where the local island newsheet recorded her temporary transformation from a ketch to a cutter.

Although *Asgard's* rig already seemed archaic to most sailing folk, it appeared only natural and proper to one group of sailors who regularly joined her in those early days, the members of the Howth 17ft Class of 1898 vintage. Even today, they still sail their boats exactly as originally designed, and back in 1969-74, their experience in racing with gaff rig helped *Asgard* to success, for

Asgard making good speed in the style which won her first STA race. Gaff rig enthusiasts from the Howth 17 class had been brought aboard to optimise the setting of the tops'l.

Colin Archer had designed one mighty slippy boat. Howth 17 sailors including Cyril Geran, Aideen McHenry, Brendan Cassidy, and Bryan and Mark Lynch, had been invited aboard early in the 1969 season to assist in the first setting of *Asgard's* topsail during her sail training career, and later they were among those who helped the old girl towards racing victory. In 1971 with her racing rig improved with a newly-made traditional-style "leg o'mutton" spinnaker, she was on top form with wins in the STA's Weymouth to St Malo and Plymouth to Cherbourg races.

The creation of that new race-winning spin-naker gives some indica-tion of the way that *Asgard*

Gliding along under the new spinnaker

had to be run in order to stay within budget. The boom was provided free by a firm of builders' suppliers in Dun Laoghaire. The fittings were made as a training exercise by apprentices in the CIE workshops courtesy of Frank Lemass. And the making of the spinnaker itself was personally supervised by one of the keenest and most able of *Asgard* volunteer skippers, Lew Heath, who just happened to be the manager of Perry's sail-loft in Dun Laoghaire.

In today's more structured and "professionalised" world, such a level of amateur enthusiasm is inconceivable. Indeed, it would arguably be a nuisance. But back in 1971, that's the way it was with *Asgard*. Yet by the end of the 1972 season, the writing was already on the wall for the old ketch's days as Ireland's sail training vessel. With entry to the European Economic Community (now the EU) in 1972, Ireland had launched into change. So when the *Asgard* went to the Baltic with the STA programme in 1972 in an intense series of races and Parades of Sail which also took in the 1972 Olympics at Kiel in Germany, it provided a symbolic and actual involvement with the heart of Europe, an experience which forcefully underlined the fact that even a small nation such as Ireland should expect to have its own proper sail training ship, rather than make do with a little old slightly converted yacht, albeit of considerable historical significance.

91

Be that as it may, *Asgard* did her utmost in 1972 as she returned to the waters she sailed with Erskine and Molly Childers in 1906 and again in 1913. Some 59 years later, perhaps the most memorable visit was to the north German port of Travemunde, which was reached after a cruise-in-company from Malmo in Sweden, complete with crew changing experience for the Irish trainees with the Norwegian square-rigged ship *Christian Radich,* the Polish schooner *Zawisza,* the US Coastguard barque *Eagle,* the Danish merchant navy training ship *Danmark,* and two French vessels, the cutter *Glenans* and the schooner *Belle Poule.*

Despite it being 0500 hrs when *Asgard* entered Travemunde, there was a large crowd on the pier to welcome the arriving fleet, and the Irish vessel was allocated the services of Heinrich, a German teenager, as "ship's friend". He fulfilled his duties with efficiency and style despite being immediately called 'Henry' by *Asgard's* crew, though he took a special pleasure in getting the trainees out of their bunks to play a football match at 0800 hrs..

From the midst of this fun and festivity, Eric Healy went to the nearby city of Lubeck for a particularly poignant church service. In the church in Lubeck is the sole surviving lifeboat from the *Pamir.* The mighty 275ft square rigger, aboard which Daphne French and Betty Parsons had sailed from Dublin to Australia in 1935-36, had been recommissioned by the Germans in 1955. She and her sister-ship *Passat* had begun new careers as cargo-carrying sail training ships, with a large part of their crew being cadets for the German Merchant Marine between the ages of 16 and 18. The venture had gone well, and both vessels had frequently rounded Cape Horn.

So it was cruelly ironic that, in September 1957 while on a passage from Buenos Aires to Hamburg with a cargo of more than 3,000 tons of barley in her sixteenth round trip in her new role, the *Pamir* was overwhelmed by a rogue hurricane which had moved rapidly northwest from its area of origin near the Cape Verde Islands, instead of following the usual westerly track of Atlantic tropical disturbances. The *Pamir* was struck by the full force of the sudden storm in the normally gentle waters 500 miles southwest of the Azores on the evening of September 20th. She took on a 30 degree list which may have been caused by faulty stowage of the cargo, as there had been a dock strike in Buenos Aires, and the ship had been loaded by army conscripts. By the following morning – September 21st – she was heeling to 40 degrees, and then she suddenly capsized and foundered, and only one of her lifeboats managed to get clear away.

Of the 35 permanent crew and 51 cadets, only six survived. At the commemoration service in Lubeck in 1972, four sailors from the German sail training ship *Gorch Foch* stood rigidly to attention round that last lifeboat, their rifles pointed downwards. Around the font in the church were black rosettes, one for each of the 80 crewmembers and cadets who had lost their lives in the disaster. It was a powerful reminder of the ultimately awesome power of the sea.

Yet in the southern Baltic, *Asgard's* crew were also being constantly reminded that the sail training movement had continued with renewed purpose

The Tall Ships arrive at Kiel during the Sailing Olympics (August-September 1972) to be greeted by a fleet of well-wishers.

even after *Pamir* had been lost, and her sister-ship *Passat* withdrawn from service. New ships had been introduced, and the size of most of them emphasised just how small the *Asgard* was in such company. For although her crew had found berths through crew changes on several other ships, the little Irish ketch had only the space to take three visiting crewmembers on board from other vessels. In other nations, sail training was already on a highly developed scale, and they'd the ships and the programmes and the investment to match. So although *Asgard* and her crew gave as good as they got in the racing and the crew inter-changes and the Olympic visit to Kiel, the more perceptive were acutely aware that their little old ship just wouldn't do for much longer as Ireland's sail training vessel, however much she mattered both as one of Colin Archer's most significant designs, and as something of national historical interest.

Emergency steering in action aboard *Asgard* during the Heligoland-Dover Tall Ships Race of September 1972. With the wheel steering inoperable, helming the vessel was a two person job – one to man the emergency tiller aft of the mizzen mast, the other to read off the compass heading in the cockpit. Despite these difficulties, *Asgard* won the race.

Almost as though aware of her changing fortunes, *Asgard* gave of her heroic best in the Autumn of 1972. She departed Kiel complete with her own "liberated" Olympic flag, and eventually arrived back in Dun Laoghaire proudly flying it as a souvenir. On the way, in a very rough September sail down the North Sea, she was overall winner of the STA's final race of the year, from Heligoland to Dover. She won it despite breaking her steering gear, thereby necessitating helming by emergency tiller.

Such an achievement might otherwise have redounded to the credit of the vessel and her crew, but in fact this high profile instance of gear failure was used to reinforce arguments that *Asgard* was now too old and too difficult to maintain as a sail training vessel to continue indefinitely in that role. Whether or not she was is neither here nor there. She certainly needed a very major refit. But however extensive that might be, it still wouldn't alter the fact that she was basically too small for any longterm career as a national sail training vessel which could also serve as the flagship for the developing maritime movement.

There was a sense of history moving on at the end of 1972. In Chapter 6, we look at the story of how the mood of that time eventually resulted in the very satisfactory outcome which was the designing, building and commissioning of *Asgard II*. In terms of brutal

Starboard tack and making knots with a thundering bow wave – perfect *Asgard* sailing conditions for the final stages of the Heligoland-Dover Race.

95

Realpolitik, Asgard had already performed her function. The concept of a national sail training programme, and the need for a ship which could adequately serve it, had been proven and accepted. Thus, in the winter of 1972-73, the debate developed. It was no longer about whether or not *Asgard* should be renovated, but rather about what kind of vessel should eventually replace her.

In a normal season, *Asgard* would spend time with Ocean Youth Club vessels – here she is sailing with the famous *Duet* in Holyhead Bay in North Wales.

It was time to move on in other ways too. The days of amateur enthusiasm were being left behind, and charming old practices, such as the tradition whereby *Coiste an Asgard* met in Gibney's pub in Malahide, were quietly discontinued. Sadly for all who knew him, Frank Lemass died in 1974. He would have been well able for the new circumstances, but it was not to be. Others had to take up the challenge of keeping his legacy of sail training alive, and in so doing, they naturally introduced new management styles and new ways of doing things.

However, for the old *Asgard,* innovation was not an option. She was too much her own self for any further useful alteration, yet her place in history meant that, from being an active sail training ship, after another two years of sailing she was moved into the strange limbo of being both a former sailing vessel, and a national monument. Such things happen slowly. She continued as a

Ship's business. Eric Healy checks aboard a new crew during a changeover in Dunmore East.

sail training vessel in 1973 and 1974. But a marine surveyor's report at this time underlined the reality that hard decisions would soon have to be taken on whether or not a major expenditure programme should be implemented to up-grade the old ketch, if only to get an extra season or two out of her. The decision inclined towards a temporary replacement while the new purpose-built ship was being designed and built. So at the conclusion of the 1974 season, *Asgard's* career as a sail training vessel came quietly to an end.

Asgard's last season as a sail training vessel was in 1974. She is seen here sailing along under all her finery off the west coast of Brittany in July, 1974.

Asgard in the English Channel off Start Point in Devon in 1932, when she was owned by Major W.B.Branston, her owner from 1932 to 1937. *(From a painting by Charles Pears ROI)*

Jack Tyrrell's inspiration for *Asgard II* came from memories of sailing as a schoolboy on his uncle's Arklow-based 163-ton brigantine, the *Lady of Avenel*. Built by Trethowan of Falmouth in 1874, her home port was Arklow between 1902 and 1917. This portrait of the ship is a fine example of an "owner's picture", which were produced for the neighbourhood shipowners with speed and skill by local artists. In this case, there was just a little too much haste – the vessel's name is inaccurately given as "Avelen".

Early days of training aboard *Asgard*. Malcolm Fitzell (left, in white cap) was *Coiste an Asgard's* first trainee – he applied to join in March 1968, a year before the ship was actually commissioned. He is giving helming hints to Paula Earley, with Michael "Chinnegan" Finnegan at the mizzen mast.

Asgard coming alongside in Dun Laoghaire after day training in Dublin Bay. Among those on board are David Beattie (left), Michael Finnegan (at mainmast), Margaret Delany (centre) and Malcolm Fitzell (at mizzen mast).

Asgard in fine form in the Solent in 1971, on her way to winning her first STA Race with leading Howth 17 skipper Cyril Geran on the helm. The ketch under her stern is the London Sailing Trusts's larger *Rona*.

Asgard anchored in the Isles of Scilly in 1974.

Eric Healy (left) and his shipmates on *Asgard* drying out in Dunmore East after a tough passage.

Downwind sailing on *Asgard* with leg o'mutton spinnaker and mizzen staysail set.

Norman Long, later Commodore of the Royal Alfred Yacht Club, keeping an eye on sail trim aboard *Asgard* in 1974.

Tops'l weather – a fair wind and sunshine for *Asgard* in the summer of 1974. Yet this was to be her last season as a sail training vessel.

Gentle sailing aboard *Creidne*, which gave good service as Ireland's sail training vessel from 1975 to 1980, and continues as a training ship with the *Slua Muiri*.

Jack Tyrrell with the model of *Asgard II* and the new ship finlly under construction in Arklow early in 1980. His first design suggestions for the vessel had been created in December 1972, and he had previously produced sail training ship proposals in 1954 (see pages 24-25), and also in the 1930s.

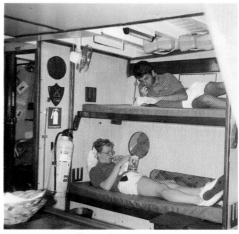

The new *Asgard II* under way. Her sweet hull was easily driven.

Off watch on *Asgard II*

A grey day at sea, but the ship going well under full sail.

The way of a ship at sea – *Asgard II* from the foremast, looking aft.

Going aloft.

Making knots. *Asgard II* revelling in improving weather during her rough passage across the Bay of Biscay in March 1985.

Far from the crowds. *Asgard II* in the island anchorage at Lundy in the Bristol Channel. The ship's annual programme tries to maintain a balance between the crowded Tall Ships programme, and the quieter rewards of solitary cruising.

Big flag for a big welcome. At the suggestion of Admiral Rothesay Swan of the Royal Australian Navy, *Coiste an Asgard* acquired the biggest possible tricolour to fly as *Asgard's* ensign during the Australian visit in 1988. Here, it makes a successful debut off Melbourne.

Asgard II sailing under the Sydney Harbour Bridge.

The Duke of Edinburgh, Patron of the Sail Training Association, is introduced to *Asgard II's* crew by Captain Tom McCarthy aboard ship in Weymouth on the south coast of England before the start of a Tall Ships Race.

The gang's all here ... the ship's company looking very trim in their crisp new uniforms in Australia in 1988.

All hands, legs over the side!!........*Asgard II* in full racing mode off the Old Head of Kinsale in 1990, with Tom McCarthy enjoying the helming while First Mate Rohan MacAllister and Bos'un Grant McEwen put themselves right into the splash zone at the weather chainplates.

It isn't always warm and sunny.

Crew aloft, putting the final touches to a proper "harbour stow".

The "harbour stow" achieved. It is only a successful harbour stow when the sails on the yards are so neatly and tightly furled that they are invisible from the afterdeck. The result is impressive, as seen here with *Asgard II* lying to anchor with yacht-like elegance on a spring evening in the peaceful creek of Lawrennie in Milford Haven in Southwest Wales.

Sunset calm, far at sea, with dolphins playing round *Asgard II's* forefoot.

5   The *Creidne* years

1975-1980

In the remote mists of time, Creidne was a sea warrior with mythical qualities of such power that she had the status of a local goddess in what is now the Dundalk region. While famous in her day, this Leinster precursor of Connacht's Grace O'Malley had been virtually forgotten until *Coiste an Asgard* set about finding a stop-gap replacement for the old *Asgard* while the lengthy process of building the new sail training ship slowly gathered way.

The 48ft bermudan ketch which they acquired in 1975 must be one of the most successful stop-gaps ever, for not only did she do everything that was asked of her – including an Atlantic crossing – while in service with the *Asgard* Committee, but today, a quarter of a century later, the *Creidne* continues to give good service as a sail training vessel with the *Slua Muiri*.

She was called *Creidne* at the direction of Paddy Donegan, whose Louth constituency included the "Creidne coast". He had been appointed Minister for Defence in March 1973 in the newly-elected Fine Gael-led Coalition Government. The change of government had seen responsibility for the sail training ship moved from what had originally been Charles Haughey's Department of Finance to the Department of Defence. This was mainly because Paddy Donegan, the new Defence minister, was the incoming cabinet's leading sailing enthusiast. But as it happened, his personal links with *Asgard*

115

Paddy O'Hara first became involved with *Coiste an Asgard* in 1973. Although now retired from the civil service, he has continued his voluntary contribution to Irish sail training as a member of *Coiste an Asgard,* and as Chairman of its Management Committee. He is seen here beside *Asgard II* at the Tall Ships gathering in St Malo, France, in July 1999 with trainee Kevin McGee (right) of Dungloe, Co Donegal.

were well established – Eric Healy fondly remembers a chance meeting in calm weather in a cove on the coast of Anglesey in North Wales. Paddy Donegan's handsome cruiser-racer was without auxiliary engine power owing to flat batteries. *Asgard's* crew were well accustomed to dealing with such problems, and thanks to the successful deployment of jump leads, *Coiste an Asgard's* work in sail training was very fondly regarded by the new Minister for Defence.

Certainly it was a responsibility in which he took a special interest, and within a couple of days of his appointment in 1973, he affirmed his enthusiasm for the concept of a newly built brigantine to undertake the expanding programme. In the event, the changed administrative structure under the umbrella of the Department of Defence proved to be a more suitable home for the developing needs of sail training, not least in that Paddy O'Hara became directly involved in the running of *Coiste an Asgard.*

In 1973, he was an Assistant Principal in the Department of Defence. He may well have had misgivings about this unusual brief which landed on his desk in November 1973, when the Cabinet indicated support for Paddy Donegan's notions of developing the sail training programme with a new ship. But, by the Autumn of 1973, Frank Lemass's terminal illness meant that the *Asgard* Committee urgently needed a new guiding hand on the helm. By 1974, Paddy O'Hara's additional duties as Secretary of *An Coiste* had became of central importance. Very soon, his quiet and steady enthusiasm, and his readiness to give freely of his own time in working behind the scenes to keep things moving along, were to become the rock on which Ireland's sail training movement is now founded. Today, although retired from the "day job" in the civil service, he still chairs the *Asgard* Management Committee, and over the years his gently reassuring presence and steadfast belief in the

Paddy Donegan's 16-ton cruiser-racer was appropriately named *Whirlaway of Oriel*.

project have helped to bring Irish sail training to its present respected status.

But while the *Asgard* project could not function without efficient administrators working quietly behind the scenes, equally from time to time the concept needed the enthusiastic and ebullient support of larger-than-life politicians in order that major decisions could be made, and in Charles Haughey and Paddy Donegan, the Irish sail training movement had the backing

117

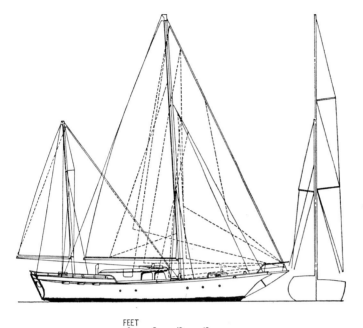

Creidne was designed by
Arthur Robb, a New
Zealander by birth, and
built at Risor in Norway
in 1967. LOA 47.7ft,
LWL 37ft, beam 12.9ft,
draft 7.5ft, displacement
l6.2 tons, engine 55 bhp
diesel, sail area
1,033 sq. ft.

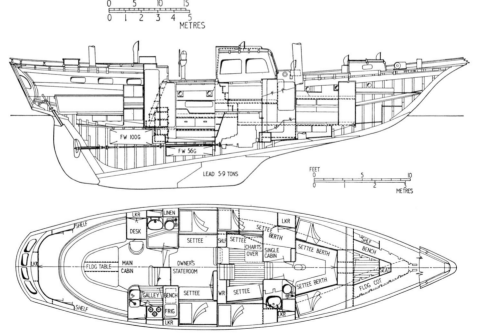

of two of the most colourful characters in national life, men who relished action, achievement and grand gestures as they battled their way through roller coaster political careers.

Certainly in the Department of Defence they'd never had a Minister to match Paddy Donegan's boyish enthusiasm for the job. Paddy O'Hara remembers a time when they'd to make an official visit to Italy to assess new training aircraft. The Minister insisted on being taken aloft in one of the tiny planes. How about looking at new tanks for the army? The Minister expected to drive them himself, and fire the guns as well. And as for testing boats for the Naval Service, why on earth have a boat-mad Minister if he couldn't steer the new craft personally?

As a TD for Louth, the Minister's infectious enthusiasm for his home territory was reflected in many ways, not least in the fact that his own handsome 16-ton seagoing sloop was called *Whirlaway of Oriel*. Oriel was an ancient princedom which had extended across north Leinster and southwest Ulster. It is still recalled in the little harbour of Port Oriel at Clogherhead on the Louth coast. In his prime, Paddy Donegan would see himself as the Prince of Oriel, and those who spent any time in his company soon realised that having a boat called *Whirlaway* was very appropriate to his views on how life should be lived. Thus as we shall see in Chapter 6, it was the Donegan delight in enthusiastic decisions which really set the *Asgard II* project under way. But meanwhile, as 1974 drew to its close, it was clear that a temporary boat was urgently needed, and once the boat was bought, Paddy Donegan was in no doubt she was going to be re-named *Creidne* in honour of the sea warrior goddess of Oriel.

Eric Healy and Paddy O'Hara were dispatched to the London International Boat Show in January 1975 to assess the new craft on display, and to use the opportunity to look at second-hand vessels at the main sailing centres in the south of England. But the boat they sought was already in Ireland. Yacht broker Neil Watson of Wicklow had on his books a 48ft clipper-bowed ketch down in Crosshaven, a vessel whose characterful looks belied the fact that she was only eight years old. Almost everything pointed to *Galcador* being the ideal *Asgard* replacement. Like *Asgard,* she had been built in Norway. Her designer, the British-based New Zealander Arthur Robb, was renowned for his seaworthy craft and his meticulous attention to design detail. So although this ketch was three feet shorter in overall length than the 51ft *Asgard,* she actually had more and better accommodation, while her traditional looks – just the job for a sail training vessel – disguised the fact that below the waterline she had up-to-date hull lines which gave her a very effective sailing performance under her modern ketch rig.

But was there time to inspect and survey this boat, and get her ready to continue the sail training programme through 1975? In typical style, Paddy Donegan met the problem head on. On a brisk morning in February 1975, a helicopter rattled its way on to a temporary landing pad at the Royal Cork Yacht Club in Crosshaven. The Minister was in a hurry. He inspected the *Galcador,* and much approved of what he saw. He authorised her purchase subject to survey, which she duly passed. With help from Crosshaven sailors and the Naval Service, she was readied for sea and sailed to Dun Laoghaire. A Springtime ceremony at the National Yacht Club – the late Frank Lemass's home club – saw the ketch being re-named *Creidne* by Mrs Vera Cosgrave, wife of Taoiseach Liam Cosgrave, and Ireland had a new sail training vessel.

By 1975 the Sail Training Association's international programme had largely taken on its modern shape, and the clarification of the rules defined sail training vessels in a generous scope. Thus provided that she had a minimum waterline length of 31ft and could pass the assessment of the scrutineers, any well found and seaworthy sailing vessel qualified if half of her crew were between the ages of 16 and 25 at the time of the race.

So although it was the great square riggers which inevitably attracted the attention when the sail training vessels gathered, in fact much of the fleet was made up of straightforward medium-sized fore-and-aft rigged craft. With her eye-catching clipper bow, *Creidne* made a favourable impact in such company. It was encouraging for *Coiste an Asgard* and the regularly changing groups of

Creidne has always given good service. After six busy years with *Coiste an Asgard* which included a Transatlantic season, she was transferred to the *Slua Muiri* in 1981, and this Irish Air Corps photo off Dalkey was taken in 1992 with Lt G. Delany in command.

trainees that 1975 was an outstandingly successful year for Irish sail training in European waters, with the new ship voyaging on many cruises and races in diverse waters, particularly between The Netherlands and Scotland.

The programme was so busy that Eric Healy had to draw on the support of Seamus Kerrigan of Dublin, Michael Casey of Galway, Len Breewood of Tralee, and Lew Heath of Dun Laoghaire as volunteer skippers, and it was under Lew Heath's command that *Creidne* made her first appearance in the prizes, getting second in the Ijmuiden to Den Helder race off the Dutch coast.

The international series in 1975 concluded with the sail training fleet gathered in the heart of London, and then *Creidne* returned home to begin the serious business of preparing for 1976's transatlantic programme. Until now, neither of Ireland's sail training vessels had ever spent more than six consecutive days at sea, but the mileage which was completed during the transatlantic season underlines the thorough preparation required, for once the STA programme was joined it became a total of 7318 miles, made up as follows:

Plymouth to Canaries (STA Race) 1424 miles

Canaries to Bermuda (STA Race) 2517 miles

Bermuda to Newport RI (STA Race) 632 miles

Newport to Galway via New York, Boston,

Halifax and St John's, Newfoundland 2745 miles

Even for a fully equipped and generously-funded privately owned vessel, making such a cruise would be a formidable proposition. But *Creidne's* management not only had to think of the requirement for regular crew-changing as part of their sail training brief, but as well, once American waters were reached the little ketch was inevitably going to be Ireland's ambassador both to local civic dignitaries, and to the large ex-patriate Irish communities to be found all along the American seaboard from New York to St John's in Newfoundland.

It was an extremely ambitious project. In hindsight, the fact that *Creidne* became very crowded at some mighty hospitable ports did no harm at all for the enthusiasm for building *Asgard II*. But while *Creidne* was in America in 1976, the new ship was still all of five years in the future. So the success of the transatlantic year in a ship just 48ft long reflected great credit on all involved, and Eric Healy partic-ularly remembers the support he received from the Naval Service, who seconded Lt Rory Costello (now Com-mander Costello) to be available for both the transatlantic passages, as well as the preparation of the ship.

By this time, too, the *Asgard* support group, though not formally estab-lished until 1983, was in effect in being in its voluntary form to give every sort of assistance and encouragement to the development of Irish sail

Creidne in American waters, with Enda O Coineen on the helm and Eric Healy and Rory Costello in foreground.

training, and it was one of the most enthusiastic of those amateur members, the late Dr Peter Denham, who deployed his considerable voyaging experience in the key role of Chief Catering Officer. While the transatlantic crews may have been hampered by lack of wind, they certainly weren't short of victuals.

Creidne gallantly represented Ireland across the Atlantic in what was, at the time, the largest gathering yet seen of sail training Tall Ships, for once Bermuda

We're here! Aboard *Creidne* in New York Harbour in July 1976, with Minister for Defence Paddy Donegan in the midst of a cheerful group of crew and well-wishers including Eric Healy (left) Len Breewood (back row centre), Rory Costello and Enda O'Coineen (right), and Seamus Kerrigan and Olivia Donegan (foreground)

was reached, the American vessels had joined in strength. With the dramatic setting of harbours such as New York, everyone involved on the Irish vessel made the most of the opportunities afloat and ashore, and it was a revelation to sailors, officials and politicians alike to discover the huge amounts of goodwill which could be engendered by a truly international gathering of Tall Ships. No-one who was involved will ever forget it.

Buoyed along on oceans of goodwill, *Creidne* sailed from the very Irish port of St John's in Newfoundland back home to the west coast of Ireland. An official reception had been planned at Galway city, but as they were a day early they dropped into Kilronan in the Aran Islands to savour their achievement. Then it was on up Galway Bay next day, greeted first by a patrol vessel of the Naval Service, and then welcomed into Galway Docks by the Army No.1 Band and Minister Donegan, utterly delighted at the success of a project which had become possible only 18 months earlier thanks to his decisive flying visit to Crosshaven in February 1975.

With the Irish sail training programme now firmly established, Eric Healy undertook research during the *Creidne* years in order to assess the effect the scheme was having on the participants. This first of three reports was written by a *Creidne* trainee who took part in the crew transfer prog-ramme while the Tall Ships were in America in 1976, and had the good

Life at sea. Christine Heath on *Creidne's* helm as Eric Healy takes a sun sight.

125

fortune to be allocated a berth on the Polish full-rigged ship *Dar Pomorza* – the second largest vessel in the fleet – as she voyaged from Halifax to Gaspe along the Canadian coast:

"An international party from five countries joined one very hot day in Halifax under the STA crew transfer scheme. We were welcomed on arrival by the Chief Officer, who gave us our watch/bunk number (mine was No. 63, Main Starboard Watch) ... Next morning we met the Captain, who gave us a talk and explained we were not to go aloft today but wait until we were sailing peacefully at sea ... At 0400 hrs first morning at sea, we line up like zombies. The Watch Leader counts us and reports to the officer. *Sagres* (the Portuguese Tall Ship) is catching us up, more sail is required. The visitors now join in with rope hauling. If there is a lot of slack the running haul is used, i.e. you run about 40ft holding the rope, drop it, then run back again and pick it up near the block, and so on until it is tight, when you heave the last bit standing ...

"We climb the mast instructed in safety by one of the training officers. Aloft, the visitors do just as much as they feel like. 0550 hrs, second day at sea, heavy drizzle, the wind heads us, all sails are lowered – very cold northerly wind. We are pulling on the ropes, one Polish cadet notes I have no hood on my oilskin and offers me a woolly hat as he has a hood ...

"One would think it would be a thrill steering a full-rigged ship under sail at 12 knots. Alas, it is electric steering with no "feel" and a gyro compass with big degrees. Too easy ... We carried on in this way for three more days, getting to know more about the vessel and her crew, until we arrived at anchor off Gaspe when we had the usual clean up and inspection. We then all went ashore to have a good time with our new Polish friends. Next morning the Chief Officer gave us a farewell beer and souvenirs of *Dar Pomorza,* and we all rejoined our own vessels after a most enjoyable week".

Eric Healy comments that many young people, while interested, simply weren't aware that it was easy then – as it still is today with *Asgard II* – to be in a position to enjoy sailing on a really big Tall Ship thanks to the regular crew-swapping programmes which have long been implemented during each of the cruise-in-company stages of the ISTA gatherings. The only qualification is that you need to have signed on to *any* sail training vessel going on a Tall Ships race, get picked by your skipper as one of the trainees involved in the crew transfer scheme, and the world of big ship sailing is your oyster. So even before *Asgard II* was built, *Creidne* could be a very useful stepping stone to square rig experience. But she also gave excellent training and experience in her own right. The following account from August 1978 follows on that season's STA Race to Oslo in Norway. Originally it had been intended that *Creidne* would return to Ireland via the Caledonian Canal through the middle of Scotland, but severe weather in the North Sea forced them southward:

"The first week was spent port-hopping along the Norwegian coast until we reached the southern tip, ready for take off. The weather – apart from the strong adverse winds – was glorious, and as soon as the tender Irish skins got over the shock, we all took on a mysterious Northern glow. We visited Morten, Larvik, Kristiansand and finally Mandal. All these places were marvellous, set in magnificent deep Norwegian fjords. The hot sunny days were spent swimming and sailing, all in a generally holiday fashion. It was possible to picnic at any time in the narrow high-sided fjords, simply by tying up to the steep rocks.

"We finally got away on Tuesday, and were met in the open sea by a wind that was to increase to a gale coming, of course, from where we wanted to go. The seas were huge, bigger than anyone on board had seen. Morale among some of the crew was soon hanging over the side. I enjoyed it, however (sailing can be like beating yourself with barbed wire – great when it's over …) I remember my first watch well. I was on the wheel, tackling the seas which we were now running before, with the two trainees on my watch sitting opposite, facing the stern. I judged the size of the approaching waves behind me by two things: (one), the length of my shipmates' faces, and (two), the velocity of their comments. For most of the trip we ran before the seas doing four knots.

"The menu was incredibly varied. On Tuesday, we had North Sea stew. On Wednesday, after some thought, we decided on North Sea stew. Just to be original, on Thursday and Friday after much thought again, we had North Sea stew. On Friday night the wind abated and I spotted a lonesome ship on the horizon. The radio sounded: "Warship *Lindesfarne* calling Yacht *Creidne* ". My finest hour. They gave us our position, and we were spot on, give or take a hundred miles! Next morning we were berthed in Great Yarmouth after a memorable trip."

The fact that stress of weather had forced *Creidne* down to Great Yarmouth in the far east of England, rather than seeing her at her destination of Inverness in the middle of Scotland, gives an idea of the sometimes un-expected crew-changing locations which the *Asgard* Office had to deal with at a time when ship-to-shore communication was primitive for relatively small craft. Then too, in the 1970s GPS navigation didn't exist, and though precise navigation was possible by experts, tyro sailors often had difficulty in believing that anyone aboard really knew where the vessel was located.

As well, to a casual reader, while the account of the pleasures of cruising the Norwegian

Making knots. *Creidne* on passage with a crew of trainees.

coast may be readily accepted, surely most trainees were put off by bad weather, particularly if they suffered from acute seasickness? Well, you have only to attend the annual *Asgard* Reunion early in January, or see the way that people regularly re-apply for berths year after year until they've become 25, to realise that the wonder of going down to the sea in Tall Ships is something so powerful that pleasant memories almost always obliterate the recollection of the hard times. This is indicated by the third account collated by Eric Healy, drawing on the experience of a training cruise in *Creidne* on Ireland's Atlantic seaboard in July 1980:

"We put up our hammocks and settled down to go to sleep. But try as we might none of us could get more than half an hour's sleep during the whole night. As a result of this when we had to get up at 4.00 am, we were all very tired. After a good breakfast, we hoisted sails and were away. From then on we were continually working, adjusting sails, coiling ropes, washing dishes etc … On that first day myself and other lads were seasick. I was one of the worst and was laid off my duties and stayed in bed until about noon the next day. By that time were nearing the Aran Islands. At about 8.00 pm we were allowed to go ashore. We went around the island and had a great laugh. At 11.0 pm we arrived back at the boat. We went straight to sleep that night. At 4.30 am next morning, we got up and made breakfast and then we were off again. On this journey we went from the Aran Islands to Foynes. We passed the beautiful coast of Clare with the Cliffs of Moher … From Foynes, we travelled back down the Shannon Estuary, down the coast of Kerry, around the famous Fastnet Rock, and along the south coast by County Cork and lastly around the Old Head of Kinsale and into Crosshaven. Then we had to scrub the boat from one end to the other. At about 9.00 pm we were allowed to go ashore to the yacht club, and when we returned to the boat the Captain took us all out for a meal in a local restaurant. At 12.00 pm we went back to the boat and to bed. The next day we were allowed to sleep until 9.00 am (it being our last day on board) … So the trip was over, and I enjoyed it immensely."

Creidne continued with this busy sailing programme in the years 1977 to

Creidne at the Naval Base on Haulbowline Island in Cork Harbour.

1980, though inevitably it seemed somewhat anticlimactic after the sheer exuberance of the American visit, and in the light of the awareness that the construction of *Asgard II* was finally moving ahead. Yet the fact that the annual programme was now consolidated was an important part of the development process, as too were the realities of living with political changes, for in addition to backing from flamboyant characters such as Charles Haughey and Paddy Donegan, *Coiste an Asgard* were in the happy position of finding that they received equally enthusiastic support from other Ministers such as Bobby Molloy from Galway, and George Colley from South Dublin.

With the planning and building of *Asgard II* taking up an increasing amount of his time, Eric Healy found that in running *Creidne* he was ever more reliant on the help of two very able volunteer first mates, Bruce Weldon and Pat Griffith, as well as his original group of volunteer skippers. Thus in August 1979 when Ireland was being swept by the gales which caused so much loss of life in that year's Fastnet Race, *Creidne* was actually sailing down Ireland's Atlantic seaboard on passage from Oban in Scotland towards Galway with the late Len Breewood in command, and in his charge the *Creidne* came through the Fastnet storm with vessel and crew unscathed. At a time when offshore sailing in small vessels was receiving much unfavourable publicity, it was an achievement which did *Coiste an Asgard* no end of good.

By the end of the 1980 season, this phase of *Creidne's* career was over. In all, she had covered 35,024 miles in her sail training duties, and as a stop-gap she had exceeded all expectations. But she was still only fourteen years old when she went on to service with the *Slua Muiri,* and so she has had a useful life since.

However, things have not been so ideal for the original *Asgard.* It will have been noted from the account of *Creidne's* post-race cruise on the Norwegian coast in August 1978 that she visited Larvik. This was of course the port where the original *Asgard* had been built in 1905, and Eric Healy and his crew made a little pilgrimage to the site of Colin Archer's yard. The yard itself had been long since defunct, but they were still able to step onto the slipway where *Asgard* had been built and launched.

In the balance … *Asgard* is craned into the yard in Kilmainham Gaol, April 1st 1979

It was a poignant moment, made more so by the fact that at the time, back in Ireland *Asgard's* fate still hung in the balance, whereas a visit like this to Norwegian waters revealed that old Colin Archer boats were lovingly maintained and actively sailed. But *Asgard* was in limbo. She was now far from being in a seaworthy state, but just what could be done with her was a matter of debate. It was ironic that the date of April 1st 1979 was chosen to lift her over the wall into the Historical Museum which had been created at Kilmainham Gaol. The Dublin wits were all too ready to point out that it was a grand All Fool's Day joke, to be putting the old gun-runner into gaol at last.

Maybe so. But with the north in a condition of serious unrest, and with the Irish economy still in severely straitened circumstances in 1979 and the years which followed, there were real constraints on any major role or significant expenditure for the old vessel. So *Asgard* was to remain for more than twenty years stored in an open-fronted shed in the yard at Kilmainham, her longterm future a matter of continuing but subdued debate.

A decidedly thoughtful assembly on April 1st 1979 at *Asgard's* "craning-in" . Included among those present with Minister for Defence Bobby Molloy TD (centre) are top brass from the Naval Service and the Army, members of the Childers family, together with Eric Healy, Jack Tyrrell and (right) Paddy O'Hara.

Gradually, the climate changed. The peace process developed in the north. The Irish economy improved out of all recognition. And the visit of the Tall Ships to Dublin in 1998 was an eloquent demonstration of the success and significance of international sail training, and a reminder that *Asgard* had been instrumental in starting it all in Ireland. Then, too, there was growing recognition of

Asgard's exceptional value as an unusual — indeed, arguably unique — example of Colin Archer's work. Public attitudes towards the old ship were being modified, and gradually the process was developed whereby *Asgard* might sail again.

At the end of 1999, it was revealed that plans were being put in train to restore the *Asgard* to full sea-going and sailing condition. This is being undertaken by the *Asgard* Restoration Project Ltd., a voluntary group of sailing and boating enthusiasts many of whom have experience in the restoration and maintenance of classic and traditional vessels. As the *Asgard* is now an archaeological object under the National Monuments Act, a licence from the Minister for the Arts, Heritage, Gaeltacht and the Islands was required to carry out the restoration work. The necessary licence was granted to the *Asgard* Restoration Project in January 2000. The Minister for Defence, Michael Smith, has indicated that Exchequer funding of up to £250,000 will be made available to the Restoration Project.

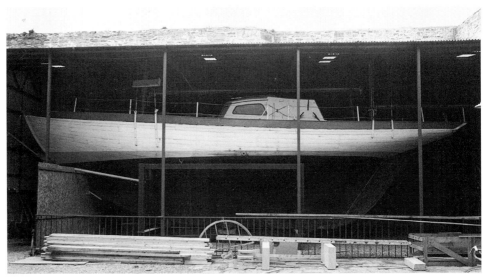

The magnitude of the task facing the *Asgard* Restoration Project is evident from this photo taken in Kilmainham in 1991.

134

6 The creation of *Asgard II*

1973-1981

When the Sail Training Brigantine *Asgard II* was commissioned at Arklow on 7th March 1981, it was an achievement which was little short of miraculous. For although the Irish economy through the 1970s had at times shown promising bursts of prosperity as the new links with Europe began to bear fruit, economic development was very uneven. Yet still the faith was kept with the dream of a proper sail training ship. At the time, life in Ireland was much affected by the northern Troubles, which were at their worst in the 1970s. However, the goodwill created by the first *Asgard* and by *Creidne* in their sail training roles – both in Ireland and internationally – was further encouragement to proceed.

Nevertheless, in looking back from today's comfort and relative peace, it may be difficult to realise that the Troubles of the 1970s so dominated life that for a period it was considered that the new ship should be called *Brendan* in honour of the seafaring saint, rather than being called *Asgard II* to commemorate a gun-running vessel, even if that gun-running had been in support of parliamentary democracy.

135

As the design concept of the new ship developed during the 1970s, Jack Tyrrell made a model which was displayed at several Irish boat shows. At one stage, it was thought that the new sail training brigantine would be called *Brendan,* and this was the name being used when the model was photographed here at the Dublin Boat Show in March 1977.

However resolving the niceties of choosing a politically correct name was only a minor challenge by comparison with finding the resources to continue. But somehow the new *Asgard* had a charmed existence. Her concept was always popular, and she was welcomed into Irish life despite the fact that in 1981 the Irish economy was in such a troubled state that by 1982 it actually contracted by all of two per cent.

So in the circumstances, the commissioning of the new ship was a remarkable achievement. Yet the most remarkable thing about it was not the creation of the vessel herself, but the nature and age of the man who designed her and built her. Jack Tyrrell was already 73 when the notion of building a new ship first became public policy in 1973. Thus he was in fact the same age as Colin Archer at the time of the first *Asgard's* designing and building in 1905.

In today's ageist world, it is instructive to consider just how totally such examples of individual creativity and energy refute the generally held views of the expected and accepted behaviour for senior age groups. In Jack Tyrrell's case, the achievement was even more remarkable. Colin Archer had a straightforward building contract with a client whose bills were being paid by an affluent and indulgent father-in-law. But the master shipwright and designer of Arklow had to retain faith in the viability of his dream through all sorts of political upheaval and tough times, such that he was 81 by the time it was finally completed.

We get some idea of the personal vitality and fascination with the project which kept Jack Tyrrell going when we talk to those who were increasingly involved as the ship took shape. By the late 1970s, the details of the rig were being finalised, and the late Len Breewood of Tralee, an enthusiastic *Asgard* crewman who later became a member of *Coiste an Asgard* on the suggestion of the *Asgard* Support Group, recalled how research visits were made to vessels like the Colin Mudie-designed brig *Royalist,* the square rigger run by the British Sea Cadets. In 1979, he and fellow committee member Seamus Kerrigan, with Eric Healy setting the pace, were given a tour of *Royalist's* rig. The word aloft was that Jack Tyrrell had been there already, a

The Colin Mudie-designed brig *Royalist,* sailed by Britain's Sea Cadet Corps, was one of several useful sources of reference during the designing and building of *Asgard II,* and for many years was a friendly rival of the Irish ship.

137

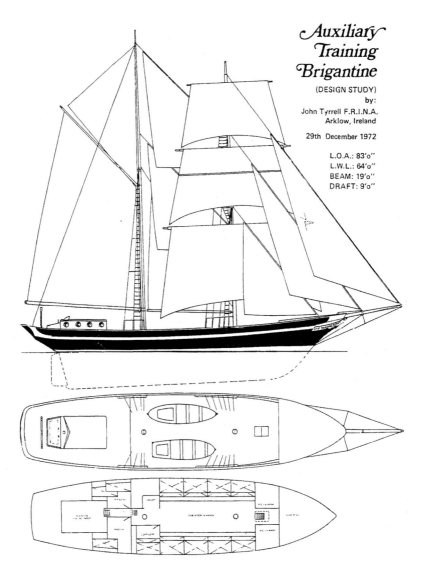

Auxiliary
Training
Brigantine

(DESIGN STUDY)
by:
John Tyrrell F.R.I.N.A.
Arklow, Ireland

29th December 1972

L.O.A.: 83'o"
L.W.L.: 64'o"
BEAM: 19'o"
DRAFT: 9'o"

The first real hint of the new ship came with these drawings – inspired by the *Lady of Avenel* – which were produced by Jack Tyrrell during the Christmas holidays of 1972. They were published in the February 1973 issue of *Afloat* magazine, and in their turn they inspired Minister for Defence Paddy Donegan to decide, on St Patrick's Day, March 17th 1973, that somehow or other the new ship would be built. The Government agreed the idea in principle in November 1973, but the ship was not sailing until 1981.

story which became demonstrably true on another occasion at much the same time in Galway, when Len Breewood and Jack were on the French tops'l schooner *Belle Poule*.

The Tralee sailor spotted the venerable Arklow man gazing up at details of the rig:

"Mr Tyrrell" said Len Breewood, "if there's anything up there you want to know about, I could be aloft in a minute and find out all about it for you, no trouble at all".

"Young man" replied the 79-year-old designer, "if there's anything up there I want to know about, I'll go aloft myself to see it. And I'll tell you something else" he added with an impish twinkle, "if we start together from the deck, I think I can promise to be there before you."

So in 1979, the schoolboy who had sailed sixty-five years earlier with his uncle on the Arklow schooner *Lady of Avenel* was still very much alive and well, relishing life aboard a sailing ship and the challenges it offered. And it was the inspiration of the *Lady of Avenel* which led to the concept of *Asgard II*. Jack Tyrrell's re-creation of the old ship as the 110ft design concept of 1954 (mentioned in Chapter 2) may have come to nothing. But thanks to the new career of Colin Archer's *Asgard* since 1969 as Ireland's first sail training ship, things were different in the Autumn of 1972. It was a long and hard road, but at its end *The Lady of Avenel* was to sail again as *Asgard II*.

Many elements contributed to this successful conclusion to a decidedly convoluted story. By the summer of 1972, the limitations imposed by *Asgard's* size and age had already become a matter of general discussion among sailing folk, even before those limitations were emphasised by the visits to the great Baltic Tall Ship ports and the sailing Olympics at Kiel. One line of thought suggested that *Coiste an Asgard* should buy the basic glassfibre hull of a modern large offshore racing ketch – the Ocean 70 was suggested – and have the vessel completed in Ireland specifically for sail training use.

Another line of thought was forcefully articulated by Dermot Kennedy of Baltimore, a leading figure in the sailing school movement who had brought the

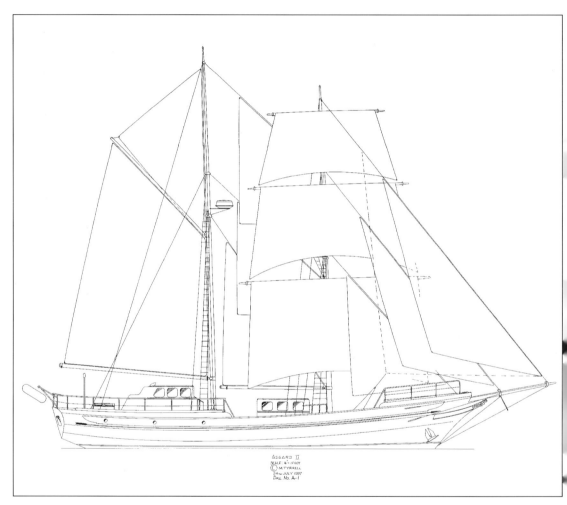

The final design for *Asgard II*. Modern requirements for accommodation meant that the deckhouses were larger than in the first drawings, but the hull had if anything become even more handsome.

140

famous Glenans sailing school ideal from France and established the first Glenans Ireland base at Baltimore in 1969. By 1972, as the Glenans manager here, he had opened a second base at Lawrence Cove on Bere Island. Dermot was too much of an individual to fit in with the growing administrative demands of the expanding Glenans organisation, so for many years now he has run his own Baltimore Sailing School in West Cork. But it was still as the Glenans manager on a summer's evening on the Baltimore waterfront in 1972 that he sketched out his ideas:

"The last thing we need for the new Irish sail training vessel" he said, "is some anonymous modern easily-handled boat. What is needed is a strikingly handsome clipper-bowed ship which will capture the public imagination. She should be around 85ft long so that she can visit all our smaller ports. She should set square sails to keep the crew busy, she should have enough room to entertain VIPs on board, and she should be painted dark green so that wherever she goes, everyone will know that this is the Irish ship."

The Kennedy comments were reported in the December 1972 issue of *Ireland Afloat,* and they were read in Arklow by Jack Tyrrell as he was winding the yard down for the Christmas holidays. After browsing through the magazine, he wasn't to take much in the way of Christmas holidays himself in December 1972. Instead, puffing quietly away at his pipe, he secluded himself in his little drawing office by the Arklow quayside, and by the time New Year had dawned, he had created an 83ft up-dated version of the *Lady of Avenel*. The

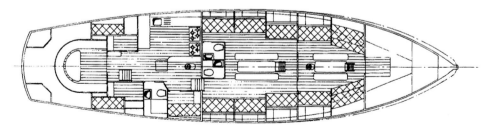

The plan for *Asgard II's* accommodation clearly indicated that although her hull was only 84ft long, she was truly a ship.

next issue of *Afloat* was the one for February 1973, and these plans were published full page in it. They were seen by Paddy Donegan, who on March 15th 1973 was appointed Minister for Defence in the new Liam Cosgrave-led Government. In typically exuberant style, on St Patrick's Day 1973, just two days later, he rang the editor of *Afloat* and announced that, come hell or high water, the new Tyrrell-designed ship was going to be built.

And so she was. But it took eight years of much hell, and many high waters, with tentative Cabinet support for the idea not being finalised until November 1973. But it simply wouldn't have happened had it not been for Jack Tyrrell's rock-like faith and determination. With the vagaries of working for political masters, he must have been near despair at times. Inevitably, too, as the idea slowly developed, his design had to be extensively modified in order to comply with safety requirements and the accommodational needs of a modern sail training ship, for although *Asgard II* may have a classic rig with a clipper bow properly finished with a fine figurehead of Grace O'Malley sculpted by Colm Brennan of Ballinteer, as far as maritime authorities and port officers are concerned she has to meet international regulations like any other proper ship.

Looking back from the new millennium, the 1970s inevitably tend to be seen as a frustrating and often drab time in Irish socio-economic and political life. Things may have started to move with the closer links to Europe after 1972, but they still moved only very slowly, and there were dark times when the very idea of something so reasonable as a national sail training ship seemed absurd.

Yet Jack Tyrrell kept quietly working away. Once an acceptable design concept had been agreed, he made a superb model of the new ship, model-making being another of his many talents. Then, without being in any way pushy – for that wasn't his style – he managed to have it on display at every possible Boat Show in Ireland. Once people could see a model, they could imagine a ship. And naturally politicos and celebrities loved being photographed with it. So the project gradually took root, and by 1977, with a

142

huge building shed being constructed beside Arklow basin, it became a real possibility.

Fortunately for its general level of acceptance, the proposal for a national sail training ship was now being actively supported by a broad spectrum of political life. Thus the Minister for Defence who personally ensured that the necessary funds for the new ship were in place at this time was Bobby Molloy TD, of Galway, and in so doing he relied heavily on the active support of his friend George Colley TD, the Minister for Finance. Neither man could be accused of being on the flamboyant wing in national politics.

Bobby Molloy.
It was the Galway TD's period as Minister for Defence from 1977 to 1979 which finally ensured that realistic funding was put in place for the construction of *Asgard II*.

By 1979, building of the ship was under way, and by the summer of 1980 the project was well on track, and it was possible to go into the building shed in Arklow and savour the joy of seeing the sweeping lines of the new vessel taking shape. She was a real honey. Underneath the accommodational additions, a classic Tyrrell hull was discernible, sweet of line and easily driven. She was built in timber with iroko planking on oak frames, and although only 84ft long in basic overall hull length, she was a proper little ship, being all

143

Can it really be happening? Eric Healy (above) in the midst of the new *Asgard* at an early stage of construction. As the ship took shape (below), the building shed in Arklow became a place of pilgrimage for maritime enthusiasts. By July 1980, the style of the new vessel was clearly apparent (above right), and Arklow's traditional shipbuilding skills were finding their finest expression (below right).

Asgard II emerges for the first time from the building shed, her immaculate topside finish a credit to all involved in her construction. Even on a dark February evening (top right), the first opportunity to stand back and admire the ship fully revealed her handsome appearance. Completion of the vessel was a busy time – the mainmast is being stepped (below). The figurehead (below right), by Colm Brennan of Ballinteer, was a representation of Grace O'Malley.

146

Arklow's pride. Commissioning day for *Asgard II* in Arklow Basin, March 7th 1981.

of 105ft long from the end of her mainboom to the tip of her bowsprit, while the hull length including the figurehead came to 87ft.

Yet again, Jack Tyrrell's faith in the longterm viability of the project was revealed, for although some of the timber needed to be imported, he had for some years been storing oak from trees which had been cut down for a road-widening scheme between Woodenbridge and Arklow. Wicklow County Council had not known what to do with this superb timber, so Jack Tyrrell offered to take it over, confident in the knowledge that one day it would sail the seas as the frames in Ireland's new sail training ship.

As far as possible, everything in her was sourced in Ireland. So although

Jack Tyrrell (left) with Clayton Love Jnr, the longest-serving member of *Coiste an Asgard*, in 1975, when it still took real faith to believe the new ship would actually be built.

A maritime dream is fulfilled. Taoiseach Charles Haughey TD formally commissions *Asgard II*.

1947 had been the last time a complete suit of new sails for a vessel setting square rig had been made in Ireland – they had been made then for the famous Irish Sea trading schooner *Nellie Bywater* by Tedford's of Belfast – *Coiste an Asgard* was determined that the sails should be made in Ireland, and they were made by Watson & Jameson of Baldoyle on Dublin's Fingal coast.

Until then, Philip Watson and Kieran Jameson had been best known for their racing sails, but they were developing a reputation for cruising sails as well, not least because Howth sailor John Gore-Grimes was carving an international reputation as an Arctic cruising exponent using a suit of W & J sails on his 31ft sloop *Shardana*. And the firm had a modern sail-loft whose extensive floor space could accommodate the new ship's large sails. But nevertheless it was quite a challenge when they got the contract. They grasped it with enthusiasm, and anyone who was there well remembers the sense of excitement when *Asgard II's* sails were put on show in Baldoyle in February 1981. For although the building shed in Arklow was by now something of a shrine for anyone who had been following the story, it was important to remember that this was to be a *sail* training ship, and it really began to come to life when you could see and touch the new vessel's heavy duty sails on the loft floor.

The link-up with the Watson sail loft has been a happy one which continues to the present day. But it is mutually demanding as well, for *Asgard II* is a performance sailing vessel which expects hard work from her sails. That she would be a performer was evident on Saturday March 7th 1981 as she awaited commissioning in the dock at Arklow, for she looked every inch a thoroughbred, the perfect vessel to move Irish sail training into a new dimension.

It was quite an occasion. Charles Haughey was now Taoiseach, and he played his part with his accustomed panache. There too were Bobby Molloy and Paddy Donegan, who had played key roles in making the dream come true. But probably the aspect which most impressed the crowd of well-wishers was the stylish appearance of Captain Eric Healy and his crew, the Captain and his colleagues in the immaculate uniforms of ship's officers, their crew manning the yards. This was proper big ship style, and no mistake. It was a long way from the make-do-and-mend atmosphere of the first *Asgard*. And it was every bit as remote from the easy-going cruising ketch ambience of the *Creidne*.

For, almost exactly a dozen years to the day since the original *Asgard* was first commissioned in her new role, Irish sail training had now come of age. The high seas beckoned.

The people's ship. On *Asgard II's* arrival in Dun Laoghaire, one of the earliest guests welcomed on board by Captain Eric Healy was President Hillery.

7   Ireland's Flagship

Asgard II 1981 to 1990

The commissioning of the brigantine *Asgard II* as Ireland's sail training vessel in March 1981 was an achievement which offered many possibilities for creative and trail-blazing activities at home and abroad. The fine new ship provided a fresh focal point and a largely unexplored range of opportunities for those who hoped to see Ireland fulfilling a more committed and enthusiastic role on the seas of the world.

For *Asgard II,* all things were possible. Her horizons could be much broader and her missions more varied than those undertaken by the Naval Service. The part she played could be imaginatively developed, for those running her and those sailing her soon realised her great potential to be a friendly yet highly respected maritime ambassador for Ireland. Embodying as she did the very spirit of the freedom of the seas and the profound appeal of sail, the handsome dark green brigantine was very soon being perceived – both at home and abroad – as a worthy contemporary flagship for the new Ireland which was gradually emerging from the turmoil of the 20th Century.

During the early 1980s, the day-to-day shore administration of *Asgard II* was carried out by Captain Michael Langran from an office within the headquarters of Irish Shipping Ltd, though of course the vessel remained under the overall supervision of *Coiste an Asgard.* This provided a significant level of freedom of

The new ship was immediately successful both as a sail training ship and as a floating ambassador for Ireland.

operation and flexibility of attitude which suited the ground-breaking approach needed to maximise the use of the new vessel. However, this linkup with the merchant marine had to be terminated when Irish Shipping was wound up in 1984. But by this time *Asgard II* was proving such an outstanding success that she continued to proceed efficiently about her business while new management structures were arranged ashore.

A smooth transfer of administration was arranged from the Irish Shipping headquarters in Sandymount, Dublin 4, to office premises provided by the Department of Defence beside Dublin's Phoenix Park. Paddy O'Hara was by that time a senior officer of the Department, but he had also continued as secretary to *Coiste an Asgard,* something which involved a considerable amount of his spare time. However, in 1983 he was appointed a member of *An Coiste* in his own right, and under his guidance a new arrangement emerged whereby the day-to-day management of the *Asgard II* would in future be carried out by an officer of the Department of Defence seconded on a full-time basis to be Secretary to *Coiste an Asgard.* This setup received further modification in 1987 when *Coiste an Asgard* was formed into a company limited by guarantee, run by a Board of Management which is chaired by the Minister for Defence, while the day-to-day running of the ship is monitored by a Committee of Management which meets on a monthly basis chaired by Paddy O'Hara.

Thus *Asgard II's* management has benefitted greatly from a continuity of key personnel which has strengthened her administration, while at the same time giving the entire operation of the ship a very human dimension. Consequently, although today all *Coiste an Asgard's* work is administered through an office which is provided by the Department of Defence, the sense of the ship's individuality and freedom of movement has been maintained, a situation further reinforced by funding assistance from the National Lottery. So though she and her crew are often called upon to represent Ireland and the Irish people in foreign ports in a semi-official capacity, it is something which can be done with an informality and lightness of touch which surely makes her more truly representative of modern Ireland than any other vessel afloat.

This overseas prestige is matched by the quite exceptional level of affection in which the ship is held at home. She is a frequent and popular visitor to all our main ports. But perhaps even more importantly, over the years her first three commanders – Eric Healy from 1981 to 1987, Tom McCarthy from 1987 to 1996, and Rohan MacAllister from 1996 to 1998 – were to show remarkable skill in getting this substantial vessel into our smaller ports, many of which can scarcely have expected to welcome so inspiring a visitor. The sense of excitement and maritime pride which infuses the smaller Irish ports when *Asgard II* comes to call is something which can only be fully appreciated through heart-warming personal experience.

The Irish sail training operation was now aiming towards a turnover of at least 500 trainees per year. With the school and college holidays coming on stream as the summer advanced, *Coiste an Asgard* knew that they had bookings which would fill the ship from the usual sources by high season. But in order to get things under way in April and May 1981, they filled the berths by turning to sailing clubs and other sea-minded organisations, as well as junior and sometimes not-so-junior staff working in the larger banks and business houses. In addition, for the first ten years of her career, *Asgard II* had an annual cruise for twenty personnel from the Defence Forces. Thus, people from many backgrounds found their sea legs aboard *Asgard II,* and *Coiste an Asgard* in turn found more of the folk they needed to continue building on the core of able volunteers who continued to be so important to the sail training movement.

However, unlike her two predecessors, *Asgard II* was required to carry a permanent crew in addition to the skipper. They included a mate (the first one was Frank Traynor), an engineer, and a bo'sun. With her complex rig, the position of bo'sun on *Asgard II* was and is a role of great importance, and the first person to fill it was Barry Martin of Galway, a former Commodore of Galway Bay Sailing Club.

With up to twenty-five people on board ship at any one time, catering was inevitably a challenge, although Jack Tyrrell had of course included a galley up to ship standards in *Asgard II's* layout. Any trainee who had become accustomed

The First Mate meets with the new ship's company in the crews' quarters to allocate duties and responsibilities.

The Great Cabin aft fulfils many functions, including officer's mess, hospitality suite, and home-from-home.

Going aloft for the first time. It soon becomes a matter of routine.

The deckhouse is the nerve centre of the ship.

Learning the skills of the sailor.

Good times aloft.

In addition to frequent foreign cruises, *Asgard II* fulfils many pleasant duties in home waters. Here, she is heading seawards with the Lord Mayor of Cork on board in order that he may comply with his duties as Admiral of the Port of Cork by casting a ceremonial dart into the sea at the entrance to Cork Harbour.

to sea life was firmly of the opinion that the permanent cook was actually the most important person on board, but as with everything to do with the vessel, the ship's cook functioned within a system of support and assistance from the trainees – it was all part of the experience.

In *Asgard II's* early years, the continuity of experience from the first *Asgard*, and from *Creidne*, meant that the ship's company usually included two adult volunteers who had sailing experience, and eighteen trainees. If they had Yachtmaster Certificates, these adult volunteers could also do navigation work and keep watch under the overall supervision of the skipper. Such volunteers, if they had experience in youth work, sometimes proved helpful as ship's pursers, assisting the permanent crew in allocating heavy weather gear, harnesses, lifejackets and so forth. However, there was growing evidence that the faster pace of life generally, and the developing professionalism of the ship, resulted in a situation whereby the introduction of new adult volunteers with each crew change was increasingly counter-productive, and the practice was discontinued in 1988, with extra berths thus becoming available for trainees.

The trainees are divided into three watches, each with a Watch Leader who is also a trainee and will probably have been selected as a result of a previous cruise and in the light of a training and assessment course. Over the years, this has become a decidedly prestigious role among the young people who sail regularly on the ship. It is no sinecure, as the Watch Leaders are responsible for allocation of the helming rota, maintaining a lookout, and working out a port rota for the duty of manning the gangway in harbour, in addition to being active and example-setting members of the crew in all aspects of sail handling and safety.

In May 1982, a new series of postage stamps was issued depicting sailing craft including *Asgard II*. She was host to a reception in Dublin's River Liffey in which other participants in the stamps issue, including the Galway Hooker *St Patrick* and boats of the ancient Howth 17ft Class, took part. They are seen here tacking up-river to berth alongside Ireland's new sail training ship.

Outward bound, and making knots. Good progress for *Asgard* in the early stages of the 1985 voyage to America.

As with the original *Asgard* ten years earlier, winning international races was good for *Asgard II's* prestige at home, and Eric Healy and his crew duly obliged in August 1981 by being winners of the STA race across the North Sea from Great Yarmouth on England's East Coast to Ostende in Belgium. It was more than just a class win – it was an overall victory. Ever since the very first sail off Arklow, the more experienced crew members had been reckoning that Jack Tyrrell had produced a swift ship, but nevertheless it was good for morale to have it so effectively demonstrated in international competition during the ship's first season.

The following year of 1982 saw the focus of attention moving across the Bay of Biscay, with the Tall Ships gathering in Lisbon, cruising in company to Vigo, and then concluding their programme with a race to Southampton in which *Asgard II* placed second. During 1983 and '84, there were training cruises to Irish ports large and small, and a visit to the Baltic when the ship demonstrated her usefulness for semi-formal occasions by being in Copenhagen during a State Visit to Denmark by President Hillery, the busy schedule including crew changing with the Tall Ship *Danmark*.

By the mid 1980s, the demands on the time of any active sail training ship of *Asgard II's* size were considerable. *Coiste an Asgard* found they had to plan their basic schedule well in advance, and with so many great ports vying to assemble the most prestigious craft, painful choices sometimes had to be made. Ever since the new ship had been commissioned, enthusiastic groups of Irish-

Americans had been try-
ing to tempt her across
the Atlantic, and it was
assumed that she would
head for New York and the
huge Parade of Sail being
planned there for 1986.

However, pressing
invitations had for some
years been winging their
way to the office from
the St Brendan Cup
Committee and its Chair-

Heavy weather in the Bay of Biscay, March 1985.

man, Commander James Ruland of the US Navy. So it was decided to cross the
Atlantic in 1985. It was a wise decision, for this enabled *Asgard II* to establish
the friendliest and most direct relationships with the many well-wishers along
America's East Coast, whereas if she had gone there as part of a vast fleet, the
impact of her arrival would have been greatly diluted. Indeed, so effective has

Biscay weather. "...the well deck was frequently full of
water, but the freeing ports worked well..."

Asgard II been as Ireland's
floating ambassador when
she arrives in some port
on her own that it has
become *Coiste an Asgard*
policy to balance the
regular and inevitable
involvement in Tall Ship
races and parades with
frequent lone cruises to
more remote destinations
such as Iceland.

The success of the

163

American visit in 1985 was hard earned. Eric Healy and his crew had to depart southward from Cork in late March in order to shape up to a punishing schedule, and they met with severe equinoctial gales in the Bay of Biscay. *El Pirata,* a sail training ship in the same area, had the misfortune to founder with loss of life, but although *Asgard II* was "lively" in the extreme conditions, she suffered no serious problems – "the well deck was frequently full of water, but the freeing ports worked well".

Nevertheless it was an atrocious Spring, and when departure westward across the Atlantic was eventually taken from Madeira, *Asgard II* was already running late. Ironically, she was then further delayed by light winds in mid-ocean, but as she was a ship of manageable size for reception committees and so forth, her hosts in America coped with the problem by putting everything back by one month. This sounds simple enough in retrospect, but there were times when *Asgard*'s administrators felt that they were dealing with a three-dimensional jigsaw puzzle in a constantly moving frame.

After a short visit to Bermuda where crew changes were effected, *Asgard II* reached Norfolk, Virginia, in late May. The time in America was busy with formal and informal gatherings. There was a reception at Capitol Hill in Washington with Speaker Tip O'Neill, and then *Coiste an Asgard* Chairman and Minister for Defence Patrick Cooney sailed aboard the ship along America's East Coast, a high point being the laying of a wreath on the grave in Philadelphia of the Wexford-born founder of the American navy, Commodore John Barry.

Enthusiastic American hosts made the ship welcome at many ports including New York and Boston, where *Asgard II* berthed with the mighty square rigger USS *Constitution,* better known as "Old Ironsides". Eventually they reached St John's in Newfoundland where a 24-hour rest was more than welcome, following which the ship had a cracker of a passage of just twelve days back to Cork and at least two end-of-cruise receptions, including a particularly memorable one in the helicopter hangar of L.E. *Eithne.*

After seventeen years of very active service, Eric Healy's time as skipper of

Ireland's sail training ships drew to a close on a cheerful note in his final years of command in 1986-87. In 1986, he commanded *Asgard II* for the last time while racing, and they took second place in the Cutty Sark Tall Ships Race from Newcastle in the North of England to Bremerhaven in Germany. They then cruised on to Denmark, following which there was an appropriately thoughtful visit to Larvik in Norway, birthplace of the first *Asgard* in 1905.

1987 saw an emphasis on activity nearer home, though there was time to visit Greenwich in London for a re-enactment of the famous 16th Century visit by Grace O'Malley to Queen Elizabeth, when the fiery pirate queen of Mayo and her hostess had to converse in Latin, as neither had the other's language, and the only tongue they shared was of the classics. A concert featuring composer Shaun Davey's *Brendan Suite* was just one of many highlights in a memorable occasion, with the international singer Rita Connolly, dressed as Granuaille, making a spectacular arrival in Greenwich poised on *Asgard's* stemhead.

Asgard II negotiates the Thames Flood Barrier in the approaches to London

An historic first meeting. The Northern Ireland Ocean Youth Club's 55ft ketch *Grania* is brought alongside *Asgard II* in Carlingford Lough on St Patrick's Day, 1987.

Before that, however, there was an equally historic meeting earlier in 1987 of more relevance for modern times, when *Asgard II* and the Ocean Youth Club's Northern Ireland training ketch, the 55ft *Grania,* berthed together right on the border in Carlingford Lough on St Patrick's Day. Since then, many St Patrick's Days have been celebrated in this very special way, and 1999 was no exception, with *Asgard II* and sundry smaller craft meeting in the lough and journeying through the ship canal to berth together in the rapidly reviving heart of Newry.

However, back in 1987 it was only a distant hope that such harbingers of a more peaceful time could become a regular occurrence. But before the 1980s

166

were concluded, *Asgard II* under her new skipper Captain Tom McCarthy had made another very significant visit, in 1988 to Australia. Early in 1987, Rear Admiral Rothesay Swan, a retired senior officer of the Australian Navy, had come to Ireland in the hope of persuading *Coiste an Asgard* to send the ship to Australia to participate in the 1988 Bicentennial celebrations. The ship's schedule for 1987 was already so firmly in place that it could not be changed sufficiently to enable her to sail there in time. But the "can do" attitude which has typified the *Asgard* story became evident yet again, and with very helpful professional advice and assistance from Captain Peter McKenna, she was shipped out from Rotterdam aboard an enormous freighter, thereby saving time and considerable expenditure, and maximising the amount of time Irish crews could spend on the ship in Australian waters.

Captain Tom McCarthy, who took over as Master of *Asgard II* in 1987, is seen here manoeuvring his new command in the London River past the Russian ship *Kruzenshtern,* with Tower Bridge in the background.

167

Constraints of time meant that *Asgard II* had to be taken to Australia on a freighter, and she was lifted on board ship in Rotterdam by one of the world's biggest floating cranes.

Admiral Swan himself had suggested that the biggest possible Irish tricolour be acquired in order to let the very large and increasingly confident Irish-Australian community know that their ship was visiting, and this simple gesture worked very effectively, that pillar of the Australian media, the *Melbourne Age,* carrying a front page photo of *Asgard* with her huge flag in Melbourne Harbour.

But in any case the Australian Irish Society, under Chairman Pat O'Rourke, were already much involved in subsidising berths and putting arrangements in place at every port visited, while the Australian Government provided a hundred air fares to assist Irish trainees towards a series of successful training cruises in each of which at least five young Australians also sailed as trainees. Captain Paddy Rahilly of the Australian *Asgard* Committee was another tireless worker in ensuring that the visit went well, while Micheal Durkan, proprietor of Sydney's Mercantile Hotel, put out the welcome mat for the ship's company in a big way.

Asgard II gave of her best in return, and in addition to winning a race against other Tall Ships from Hobart to Sydney, in her four months there she visited many of the ports along the extensive coastline between Melbourne and Brisbane, also taking in a memorable and moving visit to Tasmania, with its special Irish associations, before the race to Sydney.

Captain Tom McCarthy, the new skipper and in charge throughout this demanding programme, is a Corkman eminently suited to the role of Master of *Asgard II*. While still at school in Cork, he had been a member of the *Slua Muiri*. He had started his professional seafaring career as a Cadet with Irish Shipping in 1971, but by 1974 his interest in sailing ships and sail training had manifested itself with a spell aboard the sail training vessel *Tectona* as bo'sun. By the time he obtained his Master's ticket in 1983, Tom had already served as an officer on a

Asgard II off the Sydney Opera House.

169

A Sydney welcome for the Tall Ships, April 1988.

number of foreign going vessels, and had commanded ships of Norway's Ypsen Line before the possibility of commanding the *Asgard* emerged in 1987.

His own experiences in Australia were particularly memorable, as he used part of his time there to sit the examinations for a Master's ticket in square rig, for Australia is the last English-speaking country to offer this facility. He passed all the tests to become a fully qualified Tall Ships captain, and then for good measure, he and his bride Breda made full use of the romantic setting of Sydney Harbour to get married on the steps of the famous waterfront Opera House while the ship was in port. Then, for *Asgard* and her crew, it was home to Europe by freighter again, and a resumption of the regular annual programme which had proven so effective in introducing young people to sailing the sea, and in spreading the word abroad about the new Ireland.

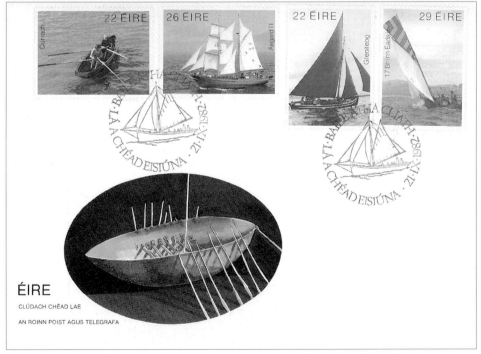

When *An Post* produces a stamps issue featuring Irish vessels, it naturally includes *Asgard II*. This is a series from 1982.

171

But now there was an added meaning to it all. For, after so many years of visiting other people's ports and taking part in other people's sail training races and sea parades, it was time to plan towards the 1990s and the arrival of Tall Ship fleets in Ireland.

Home again after another good season. An Autumn evening sees *Asgard II* coming in past Dalkey to enter Dublin Bay.

8

The Tall Ships
come to town

Irish Sail Training, 1990-1999

The popular pageant of contemporary sail training is an eloquent memorial to the faith and foresight of those who began promoting the concept back in the 1950s. At that time, while some nations had large sail training vessels which could provide an early version of what we know today as the Parade of Sail, the notion of "non-official" sail training ships, providing sea time which was available to anyone who was interested even though they might not have seafaring in mind as a career, was still very much in its infancy.

Yet today, public awareness of the Tall Ships – and what they can mean for any port they visit – is remarkably high. The goodwill they engender is astonishing and heart-warming. Far from being a parade of official stuffiness, the arrival of the sail training fleet in any port is the signal for a wonderfully informal waterfront carnival in which the most ancient traditions of the sea interact vibrantly with modern forms of public entertainment and community involvement, creating a colourful spectacle for the enjoyment of participants, visitors and locals alike.

Thus, it is now big business when the Tall Ships come to town. Major ports vie for the honour and prestige of hosting the fleet, and the annual programme

173

is planned many years in advance. So successful, indeed, has it all become that the progress of the Tall Ships has engendered its own dynamic, such that sponsors find they have become better known for their association with the Tall Ships than for the actual product they sell.

There's a satisfying irony in this, as the company most directly associated, Cutty Sark, took the name of its Scots whisky from one of the most famous clipper ships of all. For, since 1974, a highlight of the sail training programme has been the award of the Cutty Sark Trophy – originally biennially, but annually since 1988 – to the ship and crew which have best promoted international goodwill in that year's ISTA events. Today, it isn't unreasonable to suggest that Cutty Sark, who first got involved in 1972, are now more readily associated in the minds of sailing folk with Tall Ships than they are with the sale of whisky.

That won't of course particularly bother the marketing people, as they will be more interested in the perceptions of the public at large. Nevertheless the existence of such a situation is a forceful reminder of the significance of the Tall Ships and the sail training movement, and well indicates why so much planning and work behind the scenes has been necessary for the first major visits of the Tall Ships to Ireland, which came in 1991 when they visited Cork and Belfast, and then in 1998 when the fleet raced from Vigo in northwest Spain across the Bay of Biscay to Dublin.

It was a courageous decision by the ISTA to implement the 1991 prog-ramme. While Cork had been insulated by distance from much of the northern Troubles, any involvement with an attempt to reassert normality in something which had an all Ireland context inevitably raised serious security problems. As for Belfast, after twenty-two years of 'The Troubles', the northern capital had become inured to disruption. But even so, the problems of hosting an event of this nature were immense, for by its very nature a fleet of Tall Ships open to the public becomes a possible target for anyone intent on creating mayhem.

But over and above all that, the existence of a regular sail training programme for more than two decades had created very high standards of

174

event administration by the great sea ports which had greeted the Tall Ships. Ireland's reputation for hospitality and providing people with a good time socially was all very well, but there was much work to be done to ensure that the reception infrastructure was in place in ports which had never before been visited by sail training ships in significant numbers.

The Chairman of the Belfast Committee, Robin Dixon, was already familiar with the level of administration expected through his work over several years with the Northern Ireland branch of the Ocean Youth Club. But the Chairman in Cork, Ted Crosbie of *The Cork Examiner*, readily admitted that although he was a former Admiral of the Royal Cork Yacht Club and had been involved with sailing administration both in Munster and nationally, his direct experience of the needs of Tall Ships and the sail training movement as they had developed by 1990 was somewhat limited.

Teddy Crosbie, Chairman of the Cork Tall Ships Committee, at the helm as *Asgard II* races through the night across the Bay of Biscay to become overall winner of the 1990 Cutty Sark Tall Ships Race from Plymouth to La Coruna.

So he placed himself, as he put it at the time, on a vertical learning curve by sailing as a crew member aboard *Asgard II* on her main event in 1990, the Tall Ships race from Plymouth across the Bay of Biscay to La Coruna in Spain. He couldn't have made a better choice. It was a classic race, beginning with a damp beat out of the English Channel, and finishing with a storming broad reach in a sunny nor'easter which

175

Poland's *Dar Mlodziezy* racing from Milford Haven to Cork, July 1991.

was barreling up to gusts of Force 9 as the dark green Irish ship swept in towards the ancient lighthouse which marks the entrance to La Coruna's spacious harbour.

As the results were calculated, it emerged that *Asgard II* was the overall winner. She was the Belle of the Ball in La Coruna, and Ted Crosbie was left in no doubt of the kind of organisation and the necessary attitudes which would have to be in place when the Cutty Sark fleet arrived in Cork in July 1991. The Port of Cork Tall Ships Committee which he chaired consisted of people who reflected the interaction between the professionals running the port – headed by Harbour Master Captain Pat Farnan – and the enthusiastic volunteers who are essential to provide the liaison officers and hospitality accorded to each ship, the administration being monitored

Key people involved in welcoming the Tall Ships to Cork in 1991 included (left to right) Tom O'Sullivan, Eddie English, Frank Donaldson, Tom MacSweeney, Jim Collins, Ray Cawley, and Captain Pat Farnan.

by Commandant Ray Cawley, who was appointed full time Chief Executive to the Committee in the Autumn of 1990.

1991's programme began with the fleet assembling in Milford Haven in southwest Wales. The first leg starting on July 14th was round the Fastnet Rock to Cork, and it experienced some real Atlantic weather with the wind – plenty of it at times – right on the nose all the way to the rock. Inevitably the square riggers made slow progress, and some took the option of heading directly to Cork, but the racier fore-and-aft craft revelled in the windward work and one of the most famous of them, Denis Doyle's Crosshaven-built 51ft sloop

177

The variety of smaller craft which raced to Cork in 1991 was remarkable – berthed together here are *Colin Archer* from Norway, the British ketch *John Laing,* and the restored Lowestoft Trawler *Excelsior.*

The Port of Cork extends a welcome to the Tall Ships.

Asgard II's crew in La Coruna after being declared overall winners of the 1990 Cutty Sark Tall Ships race from Plymouth across the Bay of Biscay to La Coruna. The only crewmember absent is Teddy Crosbie of Cork – he took the photo.

Female empowerment.......the ladies of the port watch haul a sheet with encouragement from Tom McCarthy.

The big ships sail to Cork – it is July 1991, and Poland's *Dar Mlodziezy* is crossing the Celtic Sea, bound for Cork in the Tall Ships race from Milford Haven.

Asgard II's crew start to release the sail ties from the bowsprit as she gets under way from Port of Cork to lead the Tall Ships Parade past Cobh.

Asgard II seen through traditional rigging as she heads seaward from the Port of Cork.

The mighty *Sedov* dwarfs her spectactor craft as the Parade of Sail gets under way off Cobh.

Seconds to go before the start of the Cork-Belfast Tall Ships race, July 1991. *Lord Nelson* leads from *Sedov* and *Dar Mlodziezy*.

The British schooners *Malcolm Millar* and *Sir Winston Churchill* start the race from Cork to Belfast.

Fast sailing up the Irish Sea aboard the tiller-steered 80ft restored Lowestsoft trawler *Excelsior* in the 1991 Tall Ships Race from Cork to Belfast.

The Tall Ships gather in Belfast after racing from Cork, July 1991.

A symbol of international friendship through sail training. The flag of the Port of Cork flies above a Russian vessel berthed in Belfast at the conclusion of the race from Cork.

A trophy well earned. Oliver Pemberton (left) of Cutty Sark Whisky presents Captain Tom McCarthy of *Asgard II* with the Cutty Sark Trophy at Delfzijl in the Netherlands in August 1991 at the conclusion of a busy programme which had started at Milford Haven in southwest Wales many weeks earlier.

A neat fit. *Asgard II* is eased gently into the sea lock at Kilrush to make her first visit to the new marina in the Shannon Estuary port in 1992.

Asgard II is now a regular and popular visitor to Kilrush – this photo was taken in 1998.

1997-98 saw a new departure with *Asgard II* spending the winter months sailing in the Canaries. A highlight of it all was the mighty Christmas feast on board ship.

Visits to Newry for St Patrick's Day are a popular part of the annual programme. On March 17th 1997, *Asgard II* was floodlit in Newry Basin. The mainmast of her companion ship, the OYCNI ketch *Lord Rank,* is illuminated astern.

It wasn't all parties and sunshine in the Canaries – the good weather was also used to refit.

Baltic sunrise for *Asgard II* during the 1996 St Petersburg to Copenhagen Tall Ships race.

Asgard II in Norway's dramatic fjord scenery after the 1997 Aberdeen to Trondheim race.

Already, the countdown is under way towards Dublin 98. A meeting of minds in Oporto, Portugal, in July 1994 aboard *Asgard II* includes (left to right) Sean Flood, Robin Knox-Johnston, (President of the STA,) Captain Tom McCarthy, and Captain Fergus Britton of Dublin Port.

Blast from the past. *Boa Esperanca,* the re-creation of a Portuguese caravel (see page 6), parades past *Asgard II's* bowsprit burgee as the 1998 Tall Ships programme gathers pace in Portugal and Spain.

Asgard II powering along at the start of the Vigo to Dublin Tall Ships Race, 12th August 1998.

Mick Hunt's restored 1910-vintage Manx nobby *Vervine Blossom* making knots at the start of the Vigo to Dublin Race. She was crewed by trainees from Poolbeg Yacht & Boat Club in Ringsend in Dublin.

The timeless glory of sail – The Danish ship *Georg Stage* races away from Vigo, bound for Dublin.

A fine impression of the power of a big sailing ship is gained from Germany's *Alexander von Humboldt* thrusting her way through the seas off Vigo in the early stages of the race to Dublin.

190

Asgard II making good speed ahead of *Royalist* and *Sir Winston Churchill* in the early stages of the Vigo to Dublin race.

The fleet's in – and lit up too. Night descends on Dublin with the Tall Ships in Port.

They came in their thousands, they came in their tens of thousands, they came in their hundreds of thousands – the Tall Ships in Dublin was one of 1998's truly great events.

The men on the front line – Terry Johnson (left) and Sean Flood headed the Ships' Liaison Committee.

Tall Ships success for (left to right) Enda Connellan of Dublin Port, Eddie Nolan of Henry Ford & Sons, Vincent O'Brien of Texaco, and former Chief of Staff General Gerry McMahon.

It will be all right on the night......the fireworks display in Dublin was blessed with a dry night of velvet warmth, and attracted the biggest crowd of all.

President McAleese with the Captain and three cadets from the *Cuauhtemoc* after the Mexican ship had been presented with the Cutty Sark Trophy in a ceremony at Dublin Castle on Sunday August 23rd 1998.

Back to sea, back to work......*Asgard II* heads out of Dublin Bay on Tuesday August 25th 1998 at the conclusion of the 1998 Cutty Sark Tall Ships programme. On the foredeck are Sean McLaughlin, Secretary to *Coiste an Asgard,* and Christine Hayden of the *Asgard* Office.

Photo: Max

Moonduster crewed by Naval Service and Army cadets, made such good going of it that she was declared overall winner.

In all, nearly ninety vessels assembled in Cork Harbour, with the very largest ships such as Poland's *Dar Mlodziezy* berthing at Cobh in colourful array. The heart of Cork City came gloriously to life as the rest of the varied fleet, including some notably substantial vessels, berthed in the historic city centre, and the Cork hospitality machine swung effortlessly into action. Or at least it seemed effortless, but those in the know were well aware of the background work which was essential to keep the show smoothly on the road until, on

Asgard II starts heading downriver from Cork to lead the Parade of Sail past Cobh.

Saturday July 20th, the visit was climaxed with a Parade of Sail down the harbour past Cobh's famous waterfront. Captain Tom McCarthy and his crew on the flagship *Asgard II* led a mighty fleet which was saluted by firefloats spraying, and tens of thousands of spectators ashore and afloat on an incredibly motley fleet.

Outside the harbour, the starting line was in place for the second stage, an unprecedented race from Cork directly to Belfast. Winds were light at first, but at least the weather was sunny. Then as the fleet made its way up the Irish Sea, a new weather system brought in a lively if damp sou'easter which soon had vessels of all types piling on the knots, and they swept into Belfast Docks to a rapturous welcome with the same entertaining mixture of official civic happenings and less formal but equally impressive free lance hospitality. Belfast came warmly to life, everyone had themselves a ball, and then on July 25th they'd a Parade of Sail down the natural amphitheatre of Belfast Lough, following which the fleet cruised through the beautiful waters of Scotland and re-assembled in Aberdeen.

The final stage was another race across the North Sea to Delfzijl in the Netherlands. The crews of *Asgard II* had been so busy with their duties as flagship to the fleet in Ireland that racing had not been their first priority in the earlier stages, but they got themselves back in the frame for the final stage and were contemplating a satisfactory result when the prize-giving revealed that the rest of the fleet had other things in mind for them. For, in Delfzijl, it was announced that *Asgard II* was the 1991 winner of the Cutty Sark Trophy for the ship and crew adjudged by other captains and crews to have best exemplified international goodwill during the summer's programme.

Barely ten years earlier, *Asgard II* had been commissioned for the first time. Yet now, despite the continuing agony of the Troubles in Ireland, here she was putting Ireland right at the heart of international goodwill and the peaceful message of the sail training movement. It was a stunning achievement. Her predecessors on the list of winners read like a Who's Who of all that was best in this "new" style of seafaring, for they were Russia's *Kruzenshtern* (1974),

196

Home again with the Cutty Sark Trophy at the end of the 1991 season, *Asgard II's* permanent crew are (left to right) Rohan MacAllister (First Mate), Barry Martin (Bos'un), Chief Engineer David Kerr, Captain Tom McCarthy, and Catering Officer Annie Goulding.

Belgium's *Zenobe Gramme* (1976), Sweden's *Gladan* (1978), Poland's *Dar Pomorza* (1980), The Netherlands' *Urania* (1982), Britain's *Sir Winston Churchill* (1984), Sweden's *Atlantica av Giothenburg* (1986), *Urania* again in 1988, Poland's *Iskra* in 1989 when the award became annual, and Denmark's *Hans Krogh* in 1990. In such company, *Asgard II* was at home.

Through the remainder of the 1990s, *Asgard II* activity was typical of the world's busier sail training vessels, but with that special Irish flavour which adds

Despite a busy international programme, *Asgard II* also continued with extensive cruising on the Irish coast. A particularly memorable occasion was her first visit to the new marina at Kilrush on the Shannon Estuary in 1992, where two local trainees joined the crew. They are Kilrush Community School students Aine Considine (17, left) and 16-year-old Donal Minihan (right) on board ship with Michael Houlihan, Chairman of Shannon Development.

197

Ever since 1977, a highlight of the annual *Asgard* Reunion in January has been the award of trophies to the Trainee of the Year, and the Watch Leader of the Year. Seen at the Reunion on January 8th 1993 are (left to right) Noel Dempsey TD, Minister of State at the Departments of An Taoiseach and Defence, Bernie Ni Ghaoithin of Galway, 1992 Trainee of the Year, Sarah Murphy of Dublin, Watch Leader of the Year, and Captain Tom McCarthy.

Sean Barrett TD, Minister for Defence (left), with the 1996 Trainee of the Year Louise Moynihan, and Gabriel Bradley, Secretary to *Coiste an Asgard* from 1991 to 1998.

The 1995 *Asgard* Reunion saw Dr Penelope Bleakley (right) being awarded the *Asgard* "Person of the Year" trophy in recognition of her voluntary work for the ship.
She is with Farran McKay (left) 1994 Trainee of the Year, and Niamh McGlynn, Watch Leader of the Year. Penny Bleakley had herself been Trainee of the Year in 1980.

Captain Rohan MacAllister and his wife Niamh, receive a presentation from Minister for Defence, Michael Smith TD, in recognition of his successful command of the ship from 1996 to 1999, and his service as First Mate from 1988 to 1996.

so much to her success, with as many visits as possible to Irish ports always being a priority. After nine busy years, Captain Tom McCarthy in 1996 handed over the post of regular captain to Rohan MacAllister, who had joined the ship as Mate in 1988. Appropriately, he had heard for the first time that there was a vacancy while dealing with mail awaiting him in the famous Cafe Sport in Horta in the Azores in May 1988. At the time, he was competing with his brother Brian in a three stage west to east two-handed Transatlantic Race, which was to finish at Gibraltar. Although racing one of the smallest boats, the Nicholson 32 sloop *Sea Spell*, the brothers MacAllister were doing mighty well in the race. But as it happened, the letter from Rohan's mother told him that she had actually already applied for the job on his behalf. So Rohan phoned home to ask if the position could be put on hold while he sailed the final leg to Gibraltar. The *Asgard* Office duly obliged, the MacAllister brothers got themselves an excellent second place overall, and *Asgard II* got herself a highly experienced mate who went on to be an excellent skipper.

Throughout the 1990s, the pace was quickening as the political map of Europe changed to improve accessibility, and the visits of sail training ships became a matter of increasing pride to the great port cities. A classic case in point was magnificent St Petersburg in 1996. *Asgard II* had never before penetrated so far into the Baltic, but she took it all in her stride, and St Petersburg was splendid with the Tall Ships in port. Afterwards, a cruise along the south coast of Finland to the Aland Islands — home of the legendary

Splendid ships on the Baltic Sea, summer of 1996. Aboard *Asgard II* at the start of the Tall Ships Race from St Petersburg to Copenhagen.

Christmas sunshine – *Asgard II* sailing in the Canaries, January 1998.

Eriksson wind-jammer fleet of Australian grain race fame – put a special seal on a remarkable season which made thoughts of the Tall Ships coming to Dublin top of the agenda.

For while Europe and the world may have seen notable changes being consolidated during the 1990s, with the Iron Curtain becoming a hazy memory, Ireland in general – and Dublin in particular – had been changing at an even greater speed. The "Celtic Tiger" may have become an over-used phrase, but the reality of it meant that Dublin was vibrant with the confidence of new wealth and energy and its extraordinary status as one of the world's favourite weekend cities. And the new buzz wasn't just a feature of the weekends, for the old city by the Liffey had become a major global destination on a 365-days-a-year basis.

Inevitably, this meant the citizens tended to take for granted the presence of large numbers of visitors in their town. By the late 1990s, they were if anything becoming rather *blasé* about it all at best, and indifferent or even slightly hostile at worst. So anyone trying to promote a sense of excitement in the late 1990s about something like a Tall Ships visit in the prime holiday month of August had an uphill struggle. For it's considered unstylish among Dubliners to be seen in town during August. If you want to contact Dublin's key decision makers, the top movers and shakers, during August, then you expect to find them in West Cork or Kerry or Connemara or Donegal. You certainly don't expect to find them in their offices ready to act immediately on emergency requests for services or funds or whatever.

As if that weren't enough, before the Tall Ships were due in August 1998, much of the summer's "official" resources for receiving visitors were being absorbed by the opening stage of the *Tour de France,* coming to Ireland for the first time ever in July. With its populist image and strong European connotations, the *Tour de France* was earmarked for significant public expenditure and governmental enthusiasm. However, while its reportage produced attractive video footage of the Irish countryside for global consumption, the impression was that it gave little if anything to the towns it raced through, for it seemed to come and go in seconds. The experience of it all left decidedly mixed feelings, and many people were wishing for nothing more than a quiet second half to the summer with no hassle and no visitors.

Bruce Lyster, Chairman of the Dublin 1998 Tall Ships Committee, with Commandant Tony Kelly and the men of 11 Field Engineers Company (FCA) after the successful installation of a Bailey Bridge to provide direct pedestrian access between Ringsend and the South Quays, August 1998.

Yet even as the *Tour de France* was being consigned to forgettable history, the Tall Ships were swinging into their 1998 Cutty Sark Races which were going to bring them to Dublin in barely a month's time. *Asgard II* had already had a busy year – for the first time, she'd spent the winter season based in the Canaries. While this new departure had not been without the occasional glitch, the lengthening of the ship's active year had been generally a success, never more so than over the Christmas holiday period. Gabriel Bradley, the *Asgard* Secretary, had thought beforehand that with the Irish fondness for Christmas at home, he'd have difficulty filling all the berths in the prime holiday fortnight. He needn't have worried. It turned out that for *Asgard* enthusiasts, Christmas aboard the ship *was* Christmas at home. So many applied that they could have filled five *Asgard IIs* at Christmas 1997.

Back in Dublin meanwhile, the places in the organisational structure which was evolving to welcome the Tall Ships in August 1998 were also being filled. Chairmanship of the Steering Committee devolved on Bruce Lyster, a former Commodore of the Royal St George Yacht Club, and he headed an inevitably complex organisation which, as in Cork, saw a dynamic interaction between professionals and voluntary workers, with John Kelly being appointed as fulltime Director working from an office in the Dublin Chamber of Commerce headquarters, an appropriate setting as Dublin Chamber of Commerce originated from an organisation which came into being when the funds from the merchant ship known as the Ousel Galley were disbursed in 1695.

On the waterfront, the professionals were headed by the Chief Executive of Dublin Port, Captain Enda Connellan, whose team had to resolve between the problems raised by the expectations of the Tall Ships and their thousands of crews, and the fact that Dublin Port's new and remarkable level of prosperity and activity meant that the harbour was dealing with up to thirty-seven ship movements per day.

Sean Flood aboard the Argentinian Sail Training Ship *Libertad* as she enters Dublin Port, August 1998.

On the voluntary side, the main tasks were liaison and safety. The Vessel Management Committee was chaired by Sean Flood, that same Sean Flood who, more than thirty years earlier, had been one of the Young Turks in the forefront of the movement protesting at the Government's neglect of the original *Asgard*. He had become a member of *Coiste an Asgard* in 1993, but before that,

205

in 1987, he had teamed up with former Royal Irish YC Commodore Terry Johnson in the organisation of Ireland's most successful ever Admirals Cup campaign.

The Flood-Johnson team came together again to oversee the waterfront welcome for the Tall Ships in Dublin in 1998, with Terry Johnson heading the Vessel Liaison Sub-Committee within Sean Flood's Vessel Management Committee. In the early stages of the organisational development, they anticipated recruiting up to 200 voluntary workers, drawing on the enthusiasm of all the sailing clubs between Skerries and Arklow. But as the summer approached, the magnitude of the task became apparent, and in the end the army of active volunteers topped the 700 mark. They came from all over Ireland, and where possible they brought their own club's rescue boats with them, one crew and boat even coming from as far distant as Dingle.

The assembly of a safety fleet with experienced crews was essential, as the presence of thousands of ships' crews and even more visitors in a waterfront situation was obviously fraught with hazard. But it was equally essential that it all be done in a low key way. Fortunately in Kieran Cruise of Poolbeg Yacht & Boat Club right in the heart of dockland, they'd the very man for competent co-ordination of the massive safety programme without fuss, and by the time the fleet arrived, the necessary arrangements were quietly but efficiently in place.

The Cutty Sark programme in 1998 started with the fleet assembling in Falmouth in Cornwall, and then on Sunday July 16th they headed seaward to race the 720 miles across the Bay of Biscay to Lisbon. The classic conditions of a beat out of the western English Channel were experienced, with the crucial tactical decision being faced of when to tack on to starboard in order to get as quickly as possible to the more favourable winds in the Bay of Biscay, following which you'd expect increasingly rapid progress down towards the prevailing nor'easters which would sweep all ships south past Cape Finisterre in northwest Spain, and on towards the Portuguese coast.

With so much windward work in the early stages, keenly-sailed fore-

and-aft craft showed particularly well, and none showed better than the 1912-vintage yawl *Duet,* still going strong more than thirty years after she played a leading role in the early years of the Ocean Youth Club, which is now the Ocean Youth Trust. She and her crew never put a foot wrong, and by the time the fleet — now upwards of eighty vessels — was assembled in Lisbon's bright sunshine with Expo 98 enlivening the waterfront, *Duet* was confirmed as

The veteran 50ft yawl *Duet,* built in 1912, had an outstandng season in 1998. She began by being overall winner of the Falmouth to Lisbon Tall Ships race, and at the conclusion of the Tall Ships programme in Dublin, she was declared the overall winner of all 1998's races combined. She is seen here achieving an earlier success, when she was first gaff rigged boat to get to the Fastnet Rock during the Golden Jubilee Fastnet Race of 1975.

The Northern Ireland OceanYouth Club's 80ft ketch *Lord Rank,* seen here with *Duet* in Vigo before the start of the Vigo-DublinTall Ships Race, was chartered during 1998 by *Coiste an Asgard* in order to meet the grealy increased demand for trainee places.

overall winner. Second place overall went to Russia's mighty *Kruzenshtern,* one of the largest sailing ships in the world, which had been looking great and going like a train from the very start. And third place overall went to *Asgard II.*

It was just the kind of news which was needed back home in Dublin, where the Tall Ship enthusiasts were battling against the onset of August *ennui* in the rest of the population, and particularly among those business leaders and fund controllers whose goodwill was essential for topping-up the coffers, which drained as quickly as they were filled. Thus it is not now revealing any secret to recall that, less than a week before the Tall Ships actually arrived in Dublin, there were no funds whatsoever to pay for the fireworks display. Yet a very successful fireworks display took place.

With their success in racing across Biscay, Rohan MacAllister and his shipmates made a mighty contribution to the developing wave of goodwill which did eventually greet the Tall Ships in Dublin. Partly, this was because simply getting to Dublin proved to be quite a challenge. The fleet cruised-in-company in exceptionally gentle conditions up to Vigo, but that brought them that much nearer the rugged conditions off Cape Finisterre and far out into the Atlantic, strong headwinds which had to be dealt with before any significant progress could be made towards Ireland.

Such had been the demand for berths on *Asgard II* that *Coiste an Asgard* had decided to arrange the charter of the Ocean Youth Club's Northern Ireland ketch, the 80ft *Lord Rank* skippered by Ed Green. Other privately-owned craft had hoped to take part, but in the end just two other Irish vessels made the starting line with trainee crews on board, Mick Hunt's restored Manx sailing fishing boat *Vervine Blossom,* which was entered under the Poolbeg Yacht & Boat Club colours, and the irrepressible Denis Doyle with *Moonduster* from Cork, crewed by Army and Naval Service cadets.

Two legends of the sea – Denis Doyle of Cork with Janka Bielak of the International Sail Training Association at the Vigo-Dublin Pre Race Reception, August 11th 1998.

Thick fog on the Galician coast threatened a delay to the start of the race, but it cleared in the nick of time, and when the fleet started on the afternoon of Wednesday August 12th in a brisk and sunny northerly, "The Doyler" at the age of 78 aboard *Moonduster* was the oldest skipper participating. But as his longtime shipmate, Colonel Barney Goulding, put it, his crewmates didn't see him as affecting their average age, "for we reckon Denis to be 78 going on 20 …"

As was his custom, Denis had been one of the delivery crew bringing *Moonduster* from Crosshaven to Vigo, and in sailing at night the final fifty miles down the Galician coast, he'd noticed the breeze coming warm and sweet – straight off the land. So although after the start most of the fleet proceeded in magnificent style straight out to sea, *Moonduster* and a couple of other boats spent the afternoon and evening energetically short-tacking close inshore along the Spanish coast. They were rewarded by the more favourable night breeze showing a distinct veer to come straight off the land, and by dawn *The Duster* had Finisterre already well astern, and was making excellent progress on track across Biscay in close proximity with the Italian Navy's 92ft ketch *Orsa Maggiore,* commanded by Captain Fabio Ghia.

The fleet had been allowed eight days to sail the 700 mile course, but had not *Moonduster* and *Orsa Maggiore* been becalmed through much of the Friday, they'd have finished at the Codling Lightfloat off Wicklow on Sunday evening, after only four days of racing. In the event, the big Italian ketch swept across the line at 0352 hrs on the Monday morning, and *Moonduster* – tearing along under spinnaker in a gale from the southwest – was in just 19 minutes and 43 seconds later, an exceptional performance which put her all of 18.5 hours ahead of *Orsa Maggiore* on corrected time.

With the square riggers still at sea for another two or three days, *Moonduster* kept her win in the Vigo to Dublin race. *Asgard II* became the winner of her class on the combined times of both the racing legs, in which the overall winner was *Duet* under the command of Xavier van Elst of the Cirdan Sailing Trust, a superb performance in a race in which some of the smaller craft, and indeed some larger ones, had experienced decidedly rugged sailing all too typical of 1998's poor summer weather.

But after all the travails of getting the fleet together, and getting the facilities in place in Dublin, everything started to go right once the Tall Ships

210

had come to town, and the weather obligingly improved. Even in the great days of sail the River Liffey can seldom have seen such an assembly of large full-rigged ships, and the people of Dublin and the people of Ireland turned out in their tens of thousands to make them welcome.

Warmest of all the welcomes was for those ships which had voyaged the furthest, Colombia's *Gloria* from South America, *Libertad* from Argentina, and the mighty *Cuauhtemoc* from Mexico. Their crews responded in turn by making Liffeyside into one vast Latin American pageant. The party swung on through the streets broad and narrow, and at Dublin Castle there wasn't a dry eye in the place as President McAleese presented the Mexicans with the Cutty Sark Trophy for best promoting international goodwill.

The scale of it all was almost beyond comprehension. For instance, the

Where is everybody? Denis Doyle's *Moonduster* (left) and the Italian Navy's *Orsa Maggiore* had dealt so efficiently with the windward sailing in the Vigo-Dublin Race that for two days they sat in solitary splendour at the new berthing facility along Dublin's North Quays.

211

Captains' Dinner at The Point on the Sunday night saw 1,200 people feasting together, yet in terms of numbers involved, that was one of the smaller happenings. The height of it all was on the Monday, August 24th, when Dublin's quaysides were thronged by a friendly crowd of all ages, and the velvet night provided the perfect setting for a world class fireworks display.

On Tuesday, the summer's strong westerlies had returned as the fleet headed seaward with *Asgard II* at their head, and an exhausted and hoarse but extremely happy team of volunteers and thousands of spectators to see them on their way. Dublin Bay thronged with hundreds of boats, and though in some cases the sails were slow in appearing – for the partying had been truly heroic – it was a handsome Parade of Sail nevertheless to celebrate the fact that, some 29 years after the old *Asgard* had been first commissioned in her new role, sail training in Ireland had truly come of age.

Gradually, the big ships and the little ships cleared the bay, and the square sails headed towards every horizon bound, in the timeless phraseology of traditional mariners, for "other places beyond the seas". Looking very well indeed, *Asgard II* took her leave of the fleet and headed north past The Baily, shaping her course under sail through Howth Sound inside Ireland's Eye.

She was sailing on precisely the same waters where the first *Asgard* had sailed into Irish history some eighty-four years earlier, and she too went briefly into Howth. But it was on the most peaceful of pretexts, in order to disembark Sean McLaughlin, Secretary to *Coiste an Asgard* and Christine Hayden of the *Asgard* office, who had been on board for the Parade of Sail. Then, the green brigantine put to sea again, and sailed gently northwards in the lee of the Fingal coast, and on along the Louth shore towards Clogherhead, where she berthed for the night at the little quay at Port Oriel in a peaceful atmosphere remote from the razzmatazz of the Tall Ships visit to Dublin.

It was a harbour choice of some serendipity. For, having sailed in the afternoon where the first *Asgard* had sailed so many years earlier, *Asgard II* had berthed that evening in the home port of Paddy Donegan, whose enthusiasm as

212

The Tall Ships come to town. Even in the great days of sail, the heart of Dublin can seldom have seen so many full-rigged ships in port together.

the new Minister for Defence had inspired the Government in 1973 to make the decision which led – eventually – to the building of *Asgard II*.

The building of *Asgard II* had in its turn made possible the visits of the Tall Ships to Ireland's great ports. But now, it was time to return to the everyday realities of sail training and seafaring, and the continuing role of visiting our remote ports whenever possible. Within a couple of days, she was anchored in lone splendour off Kilcummin in Killala Bay in far Mayo, with local people aboard in delighted welcome of Ireland's flagship to a place which, while steeped in history, is seldom enough visited by any ship. *Asgard II* was back at work.

Members of *Coiste an Asgard*

1968-1973

(appointed by Minister for Finance)

Frank Lemass (Chairman)

Brian Campbell   Liam McGonagle

Clayton Love Jnr   Dr Rory O'Hanlon

Since 1973, members of *Coiste an Asgard* have been appointed by the
Minister for Defence

Annual General Meeting of *Coiste an Asgard* in Royal St George Yacht Club, Dun Laoghaire,
Thursday 2nd December 1993.
Front row (left to right): Seamus Kerrigan, Dr Chantelle MacNamara, David Andrews TD
(Minister for Defence and the Marine, and Chairman, *Coiste an Asgard*), Noirin Butler,
Harry Whelehan AG, and John Daly.
Back row: Sean Flood, Paddy O'Hara, Commodore John Kavanagh (Flag Officer
Commanding Naval Service), Clayton Love Jnr., Mr Justice Frederick Morris,
Dr Roy Browne, John Keohane, and Gabriel Bradley (Secretary).

Asgard Reunion, 7th January 1994
(Left to right): Paddy O'Hara, Seamus Kerrigan, Dr Michael
Woods TD (Minister for Social Welfare, later Minister for
the Marine), Harry Whelehan AG, Sean Brosnan
(Secretary, Department for Defence), Sean Flood and
Gabriel Bradley (Secretary, *Coiste an Asgard*).

Meeting of Coiste an Asgard in the National Yacht Club,
Dun Laoghaire, 1996.
Front row (left to right): John Keohane, Len Breewood,
Paddy O'Hara, Noirin Butler and Freddie Morris.
Back row: Pat Hogan, Bill O'Mahony, Sean Flood, Dr Roy
Browne, Commodore John Kavanagh, and Gabriel Bradley.

1973-1997
(other than current directors)
appointed by Minister for Defence

Len Breewood
Commodore Liam Brett
Dr Roy Browne
Joe Burke
Noirin Butler
Jim Byrne
Brian Campbell
Freddie Cooney
John Daly
Commodore Joe Deasy
Dr Aisling Farrelly
Dr Ray Fielding
Perry Greer
Gerry Grimes
Commodore Peter Kavanagh
John Keohane
Seamus Kerrigan
Captain Tom Kirk
Captain Michael Langran
Frank Lemass
Liam McGonagle
Charlie McGrath
Dr Chantelle MacNamara
Commodore Wally Moloney
Louis Monks
Dr Rory O'Hanlon
Jack Tyrrell
Harry Whelehan

Ministers for Defence
since 1973

Patrick S Donegan	15/3/73 – 1/12/76
Liam Cosgrave	2/12/76 – 16/12/76
Oliver J Flanagan	16/12/76 – 5/7/77
Robert Molloy	5/7/77 – 12/12/79
Padraig Faulkner	12/12/79 – 15/10/80
Sylvester Barrett	16/10/80 – 30/6/81
James Tully	30/6/81 – 9/3/82
Patrick Power	9/3/82 – 14/12/82
Patrick Cooney	14/12/82 – 14/2/86
Patrick O'Toole	14/2/86 – 10/3/87
Michael J Noonan	10/3/87 – 12/7/89
Brian Lenihan	12/7/89 – 31/10/90
Charles J Haughey	1/11/90 – 15/2/91
Brendan Daly	15/2//91 – 14/11/91
Vincent Brady	14/11/91 – 11/2/92
John P Wilson	11/2/92 – 12/1/93
David Andrews	12/1/93 – 15/12/94
Hugh Coveney	15/12/94 – 23/5/95
Sean Barrett	23/5/95 – 26/6/97
David Andrews	26/6/97 – 8/10/97
Michael Smith	8/10/97 –

Michael Smith TD
Minister for Defence
Chairman of *Coiste an Asgard*

Secretaries of *Coiste an Asgard*

Patrick J O'Hara 1973 – Dec 1984

Seamus Glynn Dec 1984 – July 1985

Luke Mulligan Oct 1985 – Sept 1989

Donal Collins Sept 1989 – Dec 1991

Gabriel Bradley Dec 1991 - June 1998

Sean McLaughlin July 1998 -

Patrick J O'Hara was apppointed the first Asgard Secretary in 1973, and served until December 1984, when he became a member of *Coiste an Asgard*.

Gabriel Bradley served as Secretary to *Coiste an Asgard* from December 1991 to June 1998.

Sean MacLaughlin was appointed Secretary to *Coiste an Asgard* in July 1998

Trainee of Year
Watch Leader of Year
Awards

These awards were formally instituted in the 1977 season, and were first presented at the Asgard Reunion in January 1978. They have been presented annually for every season since except 1987, when no Asgard Reunion was held in January 1988 as the ship and crew were in Australia.

Trainee of the Year		Watchleader of the Year	
1977	Peter Dolan	1977	Brian Comerford
1978	Colm Humphreys	1978	Patrick Lawless
1979	Ann Martin	1979	Michael Chester
1980	Penelope Bleakley	1980	Brigid Clark
1981	Robert Martin	1981	Fionnbar Kennedy
1982	Mary O'Shea	1982	Brian O'Connor
1983	Regina Looky	1983	Brian Marshall
1984	Elizabeth Boylan	1984	John Byrne
1985	Eoin O'Regan	1985	Phillip McCabe
1986	William Greene	1986	Yvette O'Connor
1988	Brendan Carey	1988	Enda McArdle
1989	Cathy Fitzgibbon	1989	Aoife McLaverty
1990	Jane Murphy	1990	Paul Tobin
1991	Augusta McDermott	1991	Lorna Kelly
1992	Bernie Wyndham	1992	Sarah Murphy
1993	Liam Beausang	1993	Charles Mulholland
1994	Farran McKay	1994	Niamh McGlynn
1995	Ross Deasy	1995	Jenny Farrell
1996	Louise Moynihan	1996	Belin Maginn
1997	Peter Lefroy	1997	Stuart Armstrong
1998	Ian Ryan	1998	Edward Enright
1999	Paul Fabricius	1999	Vivienne Steffens

Index

FULL RIGGED SHIP

BRIG

BARQUENTINE

BRIG

BERMUDA YAWL

BERMUDA SLOOP

GAF